What Professionals Are Saying . . .

"I would absolutely recommend this book to parents. It outlines the steps to successful planning and implementation while normalizing the parents' emotionally-loaded quest for answers and actions. This is a gift from a seasoned practitioner—it reflects the most sincere desire that parents feel informed, empowered, and able to form workable partnerships on their child's behalf. Dr. Steve Curtis has combined his own working wisdom with that of the best-practice masters. His reference to the work of Dr. Mel Levine is artfully done, weaving in so many useful tools that are already time-tested by experts. The emphasis on research is an excellent reflection on today's challenges to use good data to support our decisions and strategies."

Trina Westerlund
Founder, Executive Director, Children's Institute for Learning Differences, Mercer Island, WA

"This book provides clarity for parents in situations that are often confusing and forms the basis for implementing practical and helpful changes."

James T. Webb, PhD
Clinical Psychologist and Author, *A Parent's Guide to Gifted Children*

"A very useful and practical guide for those wondering where to begin to help a child who is struggling with troublesome behaviors."

Brock Eide, MD, MA
Co-Director of Eide Neurolearning Clinic and Co-Author, *The Mislabeled Child*

"This is an important book. It fills a real need and empowers parents to better understand and help their children."

Christopher McCurry, PhD
Child Clinical Psychologist, Associates in Behavior and Child Development, Seattle, WA

"This is a terrific guide for knowledgeable parents who want to be informed consumers of care for their children. It reduces the often-confusing abbreviations and 'psychobabble' that we clinicians use into practical, easy-to-understand language."

Holly Galbreath, PhD
Child Clinical Psychologist and former Program Director, Child Study and Treatment Center

"*This guide will be a tremendous contribution to parents and also educators working with children with puzzling behavior. I have not read such a brief, straightforward, usable guide for understanding behavioral issues and implementing interventions. I think that this guide will empower parents to be involved in both diagnosis and intervention. Dr. Curtis does a good job of warning parents to proceed with caution and optimism. In my 6 years as a school social worker/counselor, I have told parents many of the things Dr. Curtis mentions in the manuscript, but in a more informal manner, and I will love having a systemic guide to follow as I work with families in schools. Overall, this is a very readable, pragmatic text.*"

Corrinne Minnard, MSW
Social Worker/Counselor, Lake Stevens Middle School, WA

"*This guide is a wonderful resource for parents who have been through the cycle of school, psychologist, therapist, tutor, etc., trying to get something to help their kid. With all the fragmented data a parent would have gathered, a systematic approach to make some sense of it would be required. This guide offers that.*"

David Kirscher, OD
Behavioral Optometrist, Island Family Eyecare, Bainbridge Island, WA

"*I appreciate most that Dr. Curtis does not 'speak down' to parents, who by and large are competent people who know their child better than any professional could. I also appreciate the author's candid recognition that there are no easy answers and that professionals can disagree on approaches.*"

Larry Stednitz, PhD
Independent Educational Consultant, www.strugglingteens.com

"*The basic philosophy for helping children with puzzling behavior this book is based on makes so much sense! In fact, ALL children would benefit from an instructional program that would simultaneously build up their strengths and address their weaknesses. Dr. Curtis' psychological, problem-solving, and profile-based approaches for accomplishing this goal are sound.*"

Diana Potter
Special Education Teacher, Formerly at ASSETS School in Honolulu, HI

What Parents Are Saying . . .

"Your methodical and comprehensive step-by-step process is easy to follow and realistic to apply (I KNOW . . . having used MANY of these very techniques myself). It has the right balance of effort for results and builds beautifully upon the previous step to produce the most important information and assessments needed to take to professionals and glean a keen understanding of the complex dynamic behaviors that a child can exhibit. I cannot imagine a parent who could not benefit from such insight into their child, whether they exhibit extreme challenging behavior or are more along the conventional norms. I would wholeheartedly recommend this book to any parent who is in crisis, or to those who simply wish to understand their child better in order to provide them with the best life skills possible."

Allison Sprott

"It says exactly what I was feeling in the beginning. Is there something wrong with my son? It catches your immediate feelings and makes you want to read more. It feels as though the author really knows how I feel. This book is so positive it gives you a sense of direction with practical processes to help you work through issues with your child."

Gena Brown

"It fills a gap in the existing literature—for how to organize and identify the issues giving rise to parents' concerns. I would have enjoyed having access to this resource when I initially became concerned about my son's issues. And even today, after my son's diagnosis, it will be a tool for helping me to pinpoint new concerns that don't fit into his particular diagnosis."

Betsy Stauffer

"I really like how Dr. Curtis states that there is 'no easy answer' with regards to the understanding of puzzling behavior in your child. So many books try and claim that they have all of the answers, especially those in the parenting arena."

Regina Odermat

"This book is a veritable gift to parents embarking on a journey to understand and help a child with puzzling behavior. It is a practical guide that provides parents with an indispensable blueprint to navigate the potentially challenging world of schools and professionals to find real solutions."

Beth Morgan

"*Your approach to a very daunting, emotional, and complex journey is broken down into the simplest of terms. The information is easily understood. It gives clarity where so often there is vagueness. The worksheets and parent resources are invaluable. It's an amazing thing to have so much support and guidance in one place. This approach is empowering and calming at the same time.*"

Cheryl Besser

"*Very interesting book! It will definitely be helpful for parents looking for ways to help their children.*"

Stephanie Lewis-Sandy

"*A wonderful tool to finding help—a must for what professional to see and how each one can help. I would have had this book when my daughter was younger. It would have made life a whole lot easier.*"

April Donahoe

Understanding Your Child's Puzzling Behavior

A GUIDE FOR PARENTS OF CHILDREN WITH BEHAVIORAL, SOCIAL, AND LEARNING CHALLENGES

STEVEN E. CURTIS, PhD

Lifespan Press

Notice: This book is not intended to replace recommendations or advice from physicians or other health care providers. Rather, it is intended to help you make informed decisions about your child's health, understand alternative approaches to better health, and cooperate with your health care provider in a joint quest for optimal wellness. If you suspect you have a medical problem, we urge you to seek medical attention from a competent health care provider.

Published by Lifespan Press
P.O. Box 11704
Bainbridge Island, WA 98110
1-866-645-2470, info@lifespanpress.com

649.152

C94U

2008

Copyright ©2008 Steven E. Curtis, PhD

Distributed by Greenleaf Book Group LP

For ordering information or special discounts for bulk purchases, please contact Greenleaf Book Group LP at 4425 S. Mo Pac, Suite 600, Austin, TX 78735, (512) 891-6100.

Design and composition by Greenleaf Book Group LP
Cover design by Greenleaf Book Group LP

Publisher's Cataloging-In-Publication Data
(Prepared by The Donohue Group, Inc.)

Curtis, Steven E.
   Understanding your child's puzzling behavior : a guide for parents of children with behavioral, social and learning challenges / Steven E. Curtis. -- 1st ed.
      p. ; cm.
   Includes bibliographical references and index.
   ISBN: 978-0-9794982-0-6

1. Problem children. 2. Behavior disorders in children. 3. Socialization. 4. Learning disabilities. 5. Child rearing. I. Title.

HQ773 .C87 2008
649/.152   2007943636

Printed in the United States of America on acid-free paper

08 09 10 11 12 13 14   10 9 8 7 6 5 4 3 2 1

First Edition

This guide is dedicated to my wonderful family,
Jane, Keet, and Andalucia "Cranberry" Curtis.
I am blessed with such wonderful people in my life.

I would also like to pay special gratitude to my mother, Dorothy Curtis.
She has been a major source of my inspiration.

Steven & Dorothy Curtis
Photograph by: Jack Curtis

Contents

.

Acknowledgments

The production of this guide could not be completed without the help of a number of family members, parents, and professionals. My wife, Jane Curtis, PhD, is also a clinical psychologist who works with similar clients. She is also a trained journalist. She provided me with much inspiration, support, and editorial expertise throughout the writing and production process. My children, Keet and Cranberry, and my mother, Dorothy Curtis, provided me with many wonderful ideas.

Next, the staff and professionals at the Children's Institute for Learning Differences (CHILD) on Mercer Island, WA helped me with the initial drafts of the guide. Michele Morgan, the former Director of Training and Community Outreach, helped generate interest in the project and provided me with much encouragement. Trina Westerlund, Sandy Nutley, Kristine Frost, Ann Rosas, Victoria Chierelson, Dick Dion, MD, Steven Berry, and Cathy De Leon, OTR/L reviewed draft versions of the manuscript.

Third, the following professionals and well-known authors provided me with valuable feedback on the final stages of the guide: Mel Levine, MD, All Kinds of Minds, Chapel Hill, NC; Brock Eide, MD, Eide Neurolearning Clinic, Edmonds, WA; James Webb, PhD, Supporting Emotional Needs of the Gifted (SENG) and Great Potential Press, Scottsdale, AZ; Christopher McCurry, PhD, Associates in Behavior and Child Development, Seattle, WA; Holly Galbreath, PhD, Clover Park School District, Lakewood, WA; Larry Stednitz, PhD, Strugglingteens.com, Morro, CA; Cinda Johnson, EdD, Seattle University, Seattle, WA; Linda Warren, MD, Bainbridge Pediatrics, Bainbridge Island, WA; Lucia Petheram, DC, Eagle Harbor Chiropractic, Bainbridge Island, WA; David Kirscher, OD, Island Family Eyecare, Bainbridge Island, WA; Michele Bombardier, MA, CCC-SLP, Bainbridge Island, WA; Thomas Monk, MD, The Doctors Clinic, Bainbridge Island, WA; Marilyn Loy Every, CCC-A, Hear For Life Audiology, Bainbridge Island, WA; Diana Potter, Lifespan Psychological Services, Bainbridge Island, WA; Patricia Haelsig, CCC-SLP, Brownsville Elementary School, Silverdale, WA.; Linne Stringer, PT, Kitsap Physical Therapy and Sports Clinic, Bainbridge Island, WA; Corrinne Minnard, MSW, Lake Stevens Middle School, Everett, WA; Lynne O' Brien, Lake Washington School District, Redmond, WA; Amber Barnes, graduate student in school psychology at Seattle University; and Michael Bartone, graduate student in education at Seattle University.

The following parents reviewed the guide and provided words of wisdom: Allison Sprott, Beth Morgan, Stephanie Lewis-Sandy, Regina Odermat, April Donahoe, Cheryl Besser, Gena Brown, Celia Ozereko, and Betsy Stouffer. The ultimate test of a quality guide for parents is feedback from the parents themselves. The glowing feedback I obtained from these parents is what helped me stay positive through the guide's final completion.

And finally, the folks at Sungrafx demonstrated remarkable support and expertise with the initial design and production of this guide. It is with their hard work that this valuable resource has been recognized by leaders in the field. Dania Sheldon, editor, helped to ensure that the guide was well written and complete.

I am very grateful for all of the above people. We are all extremely busy, and it is amazing to me that there are still many people in this world who take the time to help others. Thank you all for your participation.

Letter to Parents

Dear Parents:

I am a licensed child clinical psychologist in private practice with Lifespan Psychological Services, P.S. on Bainbridge Island, WA. Lifespan is a multidisciplinary practice comprised of psychologists, a speech/language pathologist, and educators. Our mission is to help individuals, couples, and families with issues that arise throughout their lives. We provide psychological, speech/language, and tutoring services to individuals from childhood through adulthood. The majority of my clients are children (mostly boys), ages 5 through 12, who demonstrate some type of behavioral, social, or learning challenge at home or school. Many of the children I meet demonstrate attention difficulties at school. Others demonstrate oppositional behavior at home. Some may have social difficulties with their peers, and others may demonstrate unusual behaviors that are challenging to understand. Still other children may be considered gifted. The common denominator is that their parents are often confused regarding how to best understand and help their child in need. They may not know where to turn and as a result, they begin a quest for help that can turn into a long and frustrating journey.

I wrote this guide to help parents better raise their children. In this guide, parents will learn an assessment method to better understand the nature of their child's behavioral, social, or learning difficulties, regardless of how complex these issues are. Parents will also be exposed to a philosophy that will help them intervene more effectively. In the latter part of this guide, parents will be given information to help them find an appropriate care professional and obtain additional resources for further study. My hope is that the information contained in this guide is universal and will help many types of parents who have children with diverse sets of challenges. The overall goal is to help these children find the path to success so that they develop into healthy, happy, and well-adjusted adults in the future.

Whether you are just beginning to seek solutions for your child's difficulties or you are further along on your journey and still have not been satisfied with the solutions found to date, this guide is for you. Regardless of where you are in the quest for help, this guide will help your journey toward a solution be achieved in a less stressful, less costly, more effective, and more timely manner. You will also be able to speak the language of the professionals serving your child more effectively. It is recommended that this guide be read and completed as much as possible in the early stages of the intervention process. I wish you the best of success!

Sincerely,
Steve Curtis, PhD, NCSP
Licensed Child Clinical Psychologist
Nationally Certified School Psychologist
www.lifespanps.com

CHAPTER ONE

Introduction

The doctor calls the psychologist's office. "Please get this boy in to see you as soon as possible. His parents are leaving town, and we have to know right away whether he has Asperger's Disorder[1] or not." The secretary talks to the psychologist, and he finds an appointment time to meet with the parents the next day.

At the appointment, the psychologist greets both the mother and the 10-year-old young man together. The boy, named John, presents himself as a bit aloof with minimal eye contact. He says hi but in a quiet way. His hair is over his eyes, and he immediately reaches for a Calvin and Hobbes cartoon book located on the waiting room table. His mother

[1] See glossary for definition of this and other disorders.

goes into the psychologist's office and has her son sit in the waiting room.

"People have told me that my son may have Asperger's Disorder. He is bright and loves to play and build with things like Lego® bricks and figures. However, he doesn't give eye contact, and socially he is a bit different. At home he will not mind, and when I ask him to do so, he becomes very angry and yells at me. My therapist is concerned about my son. My son's doctor and school are concerned as well. Why is my child so difficult to understand? Does my child have Asperger's Disorder?"

Does this child have Asperger's Disorder? Or does the child have something else? What could be wrong with the child? Could it be Attention-Deficit/Hyperactivity Disorder (ADHD) or Sensory Processing Disorder? Maybe he is depressed. Is anything wrong with the child at all? Is he gifted? Maybe he is just a normal boy. The answers to these questions are not always easy to determine. This scenario is a common one that psychologists and other related professionals frequently encounter during the course of their daily practice. Something about a child has caused much concern, and thus, the child is referred by parents or teachers to a helping professional for assistance. Many times there are no easy answers to the above questions, since children with challenging behavioral, social, and/or learning difficulties can be very complex.

Definition of "Puzzling Behavior"

Throughout this guide, I will frequently use the term "puzzling behavior" to initially describe children with behavioral, social, and/or learning challenges. When a child is said to have "puzzling behavior," the implication is that there is something different about the child in comparison to peers. However, the term "puzzling" does not mean that something is necessarily wrong. The child may or may not have some type of behavioral, social, or learning disorder. The child may or may not have some type of sensory processing issue. The child may have a disorder or be found to be completely normal. Puzzling only means that the child demonstrates behavior that is of concern in some manner and is perplexing to understand. The word "puzzling" helps to postpone judgment about the presence, or lack of presence, of a disorder until more investigation is conducted.

There are many examples of puzzling behavior, but common concerns presented to psychologists are as follows:

- noncompliance with requests;
- overly excited behavior;
- attention or learning difficulties at school;
- delayed socialization with others; or
- angry and disruptive behavior.

Puzzling behavior can also pertain to concerns of low self-esteem, anxiety, depression, or some type of sensory issue. Other common scenarios presented in my practice are as follows:

> "My child is extremely bright and loves to learn. However, he has difficulty behaving appropriately in groups and frequently gets overexcited. When he is overly excited, he becomes disruptive and is asked to leave. His teacher wants to kick him out of her classroom."
>
> "Joseph is in the second grade, and he is so behind others in his reading. However, he loves to listen to stories and has wonderful conversations with others. He is beginning to hate school because he feels stupid all the time. Joseph is very happy at home, but when he is at school, he is beginning to act out."
>
> "Renee sits and stares at school. She seems like she is just not engaged. At home, she demonstrates the same behavior. She often does not seem to hear what is said and has great

trouble following my directions. She is happiest when she engages in make-believe play."

When confronted with puzzling behavior, the challenge for most parents is in trying to understand their child's needs. The needs of their child are not always clear, and this is the main reason professional help is sought. The child is ultimately brought to an expert in the field because the child is a puzzle for all those concerned. The parents and teachers are not sure if the child has an attention disorder, some type of Autistic Disorder, Sensory Processing Disorder, or some other type of undiagnosed disorder.

The Quest for Help

"We have taken Jill to see Dr. Dorlin. He thought that she may have ADHD but was unsure. He recommended that we see a neuropsychologist named Dennis Raling. He said Jill had difficulties with executive functioning and said that the teacher needs to teach Jill how to sit still. Ms. Morfin is a great teacher, but she says that she has over 25 children in her classroom and that there is no way that she will have time to teach Jill to sit still. We have been to a parent coach, and we still do not know what to do. Your name was given to me by a neighbor. I was also thinking about taking Jill to Anne Meyers, an occupational therapist, because I was told that Jill may have Sensory Processing Disorder. What do you think?"

Parents who are trying to find help for their children with puzzling behavior engage in a quest for help that often follows a similar path. First, a teacher of a particular child with seemingly puzzling behavior becomes concerned that something is critically wrong with the child. Perhaps the child seems not to listen to the teacher's directions or discussions. Perhaps the child acts very immature and does not make friends like the other children. Maybe the child is very active and impulsively blurts out answers without raising a hand.

To address any type of concern, the teacher will attempt all the tried and true interventions that have always worked in the past. The teacher may talk to the student about the behavior. The teacher may try giving the child rewards for good behavior. Or maybe the teacher becomes so frustrated that the child is sent to the principal's office for discipline. When none of these actions address the given concerns, the teacher finally contacts the parents and strongly urges them to seek outside help.

Once the contact from the teacher is made, the parents begin searching for answers. Often parents do not know where to turn, since most have minimal expertise in the area of abnormal child development. In most cases, the parents end up taking their child to some type of professional who is recommended by the teacher, a friend, or a pediatrician.

If treatment by the first professional is seen by the parents and teachers as effective, then all is well. However, more often than not, one particular treatment is not entirely successful, and the parents continue their quest for help by turning to another provider. Many times parents visit with four or five professionals before settling on a solution that is acceptable. Some parents may actually visit with as many as 15 professionals. Parents may also use parent coaches, who may or may not be successful. When no solution is found, parents may just give up and hope for the best.

I have seen parents embark on a quest for help that turns into a very long journey. I have seen the parents of children with puzzling behavior take this journey many times. This journey can be a long, intensive search to arrive at an adequate understanding of their child's needs. This search hopefully results in the discovery of comprehensive understanding and effective solutions. However, many times this journey leaves parents frustrated, financially drained, and without any answers to the challenges they face.

Where Should Parents and Teachers Turn for Advice?

The amount of literature and advice available to parents and teachers who are trying to understand a child with puzzling behavior is astounding. Where is a parent to begin? To whom does the teacher listen for advice? How do these parents and teachers know what advice to follow? At the time of writing this book, I searched in the *Books in Print* data-base and discovered there were close to 10,000 parenting books on the market today. In an Internet search using the search engine *Google*, the number of hits with the word "parenting" totaled 51,300,000. Many of these books and websites are directly related to advice-giving for parents of children with puzzling behavior. I also searched for related books in the field of education and discovered that there are close to 2,000 books for teachers on how to effectively intervene with children demonstrating behavioral challenges. The number of websites devoted to this topic in education is close to 16 million. These numbers are overwhelming! And, the amount of information available to teachers increases daily. To what sources do teachers turn when they need help?

A troubling issue with most of the literature that pertains to children with puzzling behavior is that the advice is either too general or too specific. For example, there are many parenting books that address how to parent children *in general*. A general parenting book may talk about how important it is to sit together at meal times and how important it is to read to your children. However, when a parent is faced with a child who has no interest in reading and who will not behave appropriately at meal time, these books are of little practical use. Other parenting books are too specific in that they may only focus on children with a particular disorder, such as Asperger's Disorder, Attention-Deficit/Hyperactivity Disorder, or Sensory

Processing Disorder. These books assume that a diagnosis of one of these disorders has already been given and/or only look at a child from a particular point of reference. The trouble with these more specific sources is that after reading the books, parents begin looking through a particular lens that may be too narrow for their situation. This viewpoint could lead to gross inaccuracies in understanding how their child really is. Most sources for teachers also fall in the realm of being either too broad or too specific. For many teachers, generic behavior management intervention strategies have failed to shed insight into the difficulties surrounding a child with puzzling behavior. These overly specific sources have also led to failed interventions.

An additional issue seen in many of the resources for parents and teachers is that most of the strategies for intervention are based on some type of remediation of the problem. Most of the interventions are targeted toward improving the areas of weakness so that the child can look and behave more "normally." Minimal attention is given to using a more *strength-based approach*, in which the goal is to maximize the child's success in life. In a strength-based approach, intervention for the child focuses primarily on building and improving on existing strengths. For example, for a mathematically gifted child with dyslexia, a strength-based approach would center on improving the mathematical ability of the child, with simultaneous focus on helping the child learn to read.

Parents of children with puzzling behavior need to learn a method for assessment that will guide them in their quest for a true and comprehensive understanding of their child. Even though there are many "experts" in the field, the parents typically assume primary responsibility for managing the information and coordinating the multiple professionals in their child's life. Parents need to be given assessment tools that will help them in their quest for answers. To be most effective, the assessment method should be usable with any type of puzzling behavior. This method should be well-grounded in research and easy for parents to use.

Parents also need a thoughtful approach to intervention that is systematic and easy to use. If parents develop and follow a plan that is well thought out, there is a greater likelihood that their child's success in school and life will be maximized. Without a systematic intervention approach, the parents may notice little, if any, progress in the targeted behaviors, despite spending much time, energy, and money in addressing them. The intervention approach that is most effective will be one that uses the specific information gathered on the child from the assessment method mentioned above. As you will learn, it is highly recommended that this assessment method address both the areas of concern as well as the strengths of the child.

A Systematic Guide for Parents

In this guide, you will be taken through a step-by-step, problem-solving diagnostic journey in order to learn how to best understand and effectively intervene with your child and the complex puzzling behaviors in question. You will be taught a systematic, thoughtful, and holistic assessment method to use in your quest for understanding the needs of your child. You will then be taught how to turn the information gathered from the assessment into a comprehensive and effective plan for your child.

My approach to working with children who exhibit puzzling behavior is described as a "problem-solving" approach to understanding and a "profile-based" approach to intervention. This "problem-solving" approach is the method that most psychologists and related professionals use in their daily practice. It is based on research obtained from the well-established field of developmental psychopathology and can apply to children of all ages. In this field, researchers have studied children with puzzling behavior for many years and have uncovered much information about how to comprehensively understand and effectively intervene with these children.

The "profile-based" approach to intervention is based on research from the field of developmental psychopathology and writings of other authors, primarily Mel Levine, MD.[2] In the profile-based approach, parents use information about their child to create an effective intervention plan that will address both the areas of need as well as areas of strength. First, the information is sorted into two parts: areas of strength and areas of weakness. Interventions are then developed for each area. Several interventions for the same child are developed, with the goal of building on the strengths of the child and addressing areas of need. By intervening in both areas, the child's progress will be accelerated exponentially.

I am skeptical of quick fixes or simple causal explanations. Many times parents are searching for the one thing that will explain all the complex behavior and concerns of their child. When parents receive some type of "label" for their child's puzzling behavior, they may be initially satisfied and relieved to find that at last, someone understands their child. However, all too often, this initial relief is temporary. The parents realize that the answers to their questions are not that simplistic. The parents then begin searching for truth again.

This guide, instead of telling parents how to funnel their children into certain categories, teaches parents the more methodical methods of analysis and intervention that professional psychologists use in their daily practice. You will learn about the field of developmental psychopathology, in order to greatly enhance your understanding of children with puzzling behavior. Finally, you will be guided to the appropriate professionals and resources, should you need additional help.

---

[2] Recommended reading by Dr. Levine: Levine, M. (2002). *A mind at a time*. New York: Simon & Schuster.

CHAPTER TWO

Framework for Understanding and Finding Help for Your Child

When is Puzzling Behavior Considered Disordered?

One of the first questions that many parents and teachers ask is whether a particular child is normal or not. Depending on the clinician involved, the answer given can be "Yes, your child is normal" or "No, your child is abnormal." In reality, abnormal or "disordered" behavior is extremely difficult to define. There is no simple definition. After years of clinicians and researchers debating the concept of normalcy, its definitions are still very dependent on people's value systems and ideology. What is abnormal to one person may be completely fine to another person. What is normal behavior to one professional may be considered pathology to another professional. In general, the more severe the disordered behavior or pathology is, the more agreement there is that a given behavioral presentation is abnormal (e.g., severe Schizophrenia). The less extreme the behavior is, the less agreement there is for the presence of disordered behavior or pathology (e.g., mild attention difficulties).

As noted before, I use the term "puzzling" as well as the words abnormal or disordered. "Puzzling" is used when a comprehensive understanding of the child has not yet been developed. Here the term only implies that something about the child's behavior seems unusual in comparison to other children's behavior. The child with puzzling behavior may have a legitimate disorder, or the child with puzzling behavior may not have anything wrong. For example, a child with puzzling behavior may be of concern because she is quiet and inattentive in the classroom. After much investigation, the student is found to have profound deficits in her ability to remember auditory-type information. In this example, it becomes clear that the child has some type of memory deficit that can be considered a "disorder." Thus, this child with puzzling behavior is found to have a disorder in learning. In another example, a child from a language background other than English has attempted to learn English for the past 2 years. After much intervention, the teachers are concerned that he may have a learning disability. However, upon much investigation, it has been discovered that many children take 5 to 7 years to fully be able to use a second language in an academic classroom. Thus, this child can be considered typical in comparison to others with similar backgrounds and is not thought to have a disorder.

In the fields of mental health, which include psychiatry and clinical psychology, professionals use established assessment systems to aid in their assessment of possible disordered behavior. These systems are used to determine the presence of pathology. Assessment of a child takes much time and effort. It is important to realize that it may not be so easy to say whether your child's behavior is disordered or not. In order to answer this question, much data needs to be collected first.

Causal Factors

Those using the problem-solving approach to understanding must realize that most puzzling behavior cannot be explained by one factor alone. There are instances when the presence of puzzling behavior can be explained by a single cause. For example, severe sleep apnea (a sleep disorder) can cause a child to be very inattentive at school. Attention difficulties due to sleep apnea can look very much like Attention-Deficit/Hyperactivity Disorder (ADHD). If someone says that the child's puzzling behavior is consistent with ADHD without evaluating the child in a comprehensive manner, then a very inaccurate view of the child is obtained. In this case, a single cause, sleep apnea, could account for the child's puzzling behavior. In reality, however, most puzzling behavior cannot be explained by one cause alone. Instead, it is due to a complex interplay of both biological and environmental factors. However, many people have a tendency to explain their child's puzzling behavior with simplistic explanations because it is our human nature to do so.

The development of psychopathology can be very complex. Psychopathology is a term that we can use interchangeably for disordered behavior. This is the term that mental health providers use when referring to a variety of abnormal emotional and behavioral conditions. The development of psychopathology can begin early in life or can occur later in life. There is often no simple explanation regarding why pathology occurs. The complexity of its development can be revealed when you look at development across the lifespan. We come into this world with certain genetic predispositions to look, behave, and learn in a certain way. From the point of conception, environmental factors begin to influence the way we develop. For example, during pregnancy, a mother may ingest, or be exposed to, a harmful substance (called a teratogen), which may affect the child's later learning. During birth a child may have trouble breathing, which could affect later cognitive development. After birth a child may encounter environmental stressors (e.g., abuse, loss of parent, bullying) that impact later emotional development. As children grow and interact with the world, an increasing number of environmental events greatly influence the way in which they develop. At every point in the lifespan, there are factors that can hinder the development of psychopathology (resiliency factors) or promote its growth (risk factors).

Thus, most disordered behaviors are multifaceted and complex. You can really see this when we look at examples of complex problem behavior. Let's suppose you, as the reader and/or parent, have a 10-year-old who has extreme challenges in expressing his anger in an appropriate manner. He has a short fuse and has angry outbursts at almost anyone. Looking back on his history, you will find that he was noted to be an emotional baby and was not easy to calm. At the same time, his parents were under financial stress and had difficulty tolerating a fussy baby. As a result, the parents would fight with each other and even yell at him to stop crying. The fussy baby was exposed to frequent arguments and yelling. Thus, he grew up not learning how to calm himself appropriately. If the fussy baby had been born into a calmer household, the later anger difficulties may have been prevented or reduced. In this case, there is no single cause for the anger. Instead, the angry outbursts were due to an early fussy temperament and a parenting style that encouraged more angry behavior.

The Field of Developmental Psychopathology

Since the 1980s, research into the causes of psychopathology has increased dramatically. Prior to this time, most research into the causal mechanisms of psychopathology was focused primarily on adults. However, in the 1980s, researchers began to look more closely at children. This upsurge in research has since generated much data and many different ideas and theories that attempt to explain child misbehavior. This explosion of data, ideas, and theories is good in the sense that there is now much more information available that can help in the quest for understanding the child with puzzling behavior. On the other hand, this banquet of information is very difficult for anyone to fully digest and use in a practical manner.

One major and extremely helpful approach that now dominates the field of child psychopathology is the area of developmental psychopathology. Developmental psychopathology concerns itself with the origins and developmental course of disordered behavior. Researchers in the field take ideas from a variety of sources and put these ideas to the test. These researchers approach puzzling behavior without any preconceived notions or particular professional biases.[3] Instead, they are looking for the truth. As a result, developmental psychopathology can be thought of as an integrative framework for understanding disordered behavior. It is integrative in that it combines all sorts of ideas to create one common understanding of how disordered behavior develops. The field of developmental psychopathology also examines disordered behavior in relation to normal development. Researchers in the field try to clarify what is normal and what is not.

What researchers have found thus far is that the development of psychopathology does not come out of the blue. As noted above, most disordered behavior is due to a number of factors rather than to a single cause. These causes can be direct or indirect, and the pathway taken to psychopathology can be quite varied. Children with similar experiences can end up with no problems or with significant pathology. Children with dissimilar experiences can end up with the same disorder. It has been well demonstrated that these pathways to normalcy or psychopathology are influenced by a number of factors experienced during childhood, including risk factors, resiliency factors, cultural factors, critical periods, developmental tasks, temperament, attachment, emotional regulation, and social cognitive processing. The prediction of the course of psychopathology is also varied. The symptoms of psychopathology can stay the same or change over time. The most important point to understand regarding developmental psychopathology is that the origins and pathways of psychopathology

---

[3] Of course, we are all biased in some way. However, the idea is to be as objective as possible in searching for understanding.

are multifaceted and extremely complex. In most circumstances, we cannot point to one particular cause for a behavioral or emotional difficulty. We like to try to provide simplistic explanations, but most often we are fooling ourselves.[4]

Research is Critical to Our Understanding

Understanding research helps us to critically analyze claims made by others. To fully understand the development and treatment of childhood psychopathology, researchers closely adhere to procedures of the scientific method. In the scientific method, the potential answers to questions are addressed in an objective and systematic fashion. Research subjects are selected carefully, and rigorous procedures are set for studying their behavior. Data is gathered and analyzed systematically. Empirical knowledge about psychopathology is developed in a systematic fashion through "hypothesis testing," rather than gained in a haphazard fashion. A "hypothesis" is simply an idea or a question that is put to rigorous testing. Systematic data collection provides a stage for scientific and unbiased analysis of data and demonstration of trends. Research is very important in uncovering the "truths" and "myths" in the causes and treatment of puzzling behavior. It is an amazing aspect of science that seemingly obvious answers to problem behaviors are not always the same as what is scientifically found to be true.

The results of scientific inquiry can be very useful for parents when they are trying to understand and intervene with their child. For example, when people begin searching for a "cure" for their child's behavioral or emotional difficulties, they will soon discover that there are many, many methods or treatments that are thought to be the most effective. There are also many proposed causes given by professionals that are purported to be the true cause. Understanding

---

[4] For other readings on the development of psychopathology, the reader is referred to the following textbooks, which are frequently used in graduate-level training in clinical psychology, school psychology, and special education: Kauffman, J. (2005). *Characteristics of emotional and behavioral disorders of children and youth* (8th ed.). Upper Saddle River, NJ: Merrill Prentice Hall; Wicks-Nelson, R., & Israel, A. C. (2005). *Behavior disorders of childhood* (6th ed.). Columbus: Merrill Prentice Hall. Other readings are also located in the resource section of this guide.

scientific research helps parents, teachers, and professionals to become more informed consumers and better able to distinguish between established methods and those that have no established efficacy. Parents and teachers should always ask if a particular proposed cause of a disorder or particular intervention method is actually grounded in legitimate research.

Classification and Assessment Methods

When parents begin the quest for understanding their child's puzzling behavior, they can take two paths. Down the first path, the parent asks, "What behaviors can I impact?" On the second path, the parent asks, "What is wrong with my child?" These are two fundamentally different approaches. The first approach is primarily focused on determining what behavior a person can affect. The second approach focuses on determining what specifically is wrong with their child.

Professional psychologists who have a good understanding of developmental psychopathology will use both approaches when they attempt to understand and intervene with a particular child. In the first approach, the behavior of concern is clarified, and specific behaviors are analyzed systematically. In the second approach, the clinician looks for specific causes of the puzzling behavior. In most cases, the clinician uses a classification system that pinpoints patterns of behavior that are consistent with certain categories of behaviors.

Theory Building

In science researchers develop hypotheses for why a particular phenomenon is occurring. Eventually, a more comprehensive theory is developed. This theory is then used to test certain assumptions. The same process can be used in the problem-solving method for the comprehensive understanding of children with puzzling behavior. When a teacher or parent is trying to understand a child, they can first conduct observations. Then, the teacher or parent can gather other types of data, such as results of medical exams or school report cards. This data is then examined as a whole. Based on the data, the teacher and parent can then develop a theory as to why a child is demonstrating a particular behavior. For example, suppose a child named Ben is demonstrating learning difficulties at school. After much data collection, a possible theory would be the following:

> "Ben is having a hard time at school because he seems to have fine motor skill delays. These fine motor challenges translate into Ben struggling to complete written language tasks. These writing difficulties make it very hard for Ben to do his school work. Thus, when writing is assigned, Ben becomes inattentive and does not want to do the work."

The Problem-Solving Approach to Understanding

Taking time to understand a human being takes much effort. As we have just explored, when we are dealing with puzzling behavior, the causes of this behavior and solutions for intervention are not always obvious. In most cases, it is best to develop a comprehensive understanding of the child by investigating a number of factors in an orderly way. As psychologists, we are trained to approach the investigation of puzzling behavior in a nonjudgmental, holistic, and systematic fashion. By using a thoughtful system, the psychologist is able to follow a sequence of steps and decision trees in order to best understand the situation and decide what to do. This process is not always so obvious to the untrained observer. However, upon closer examination, it is apparent that most psychologists follow a thoughtful assessment system that is well documented in the professional literature.

To fully understand your child, I encourage you to use the "problem-solving approach to understanding." This approach is a step-by-step procedure that helps to clarify concerns and to systematically investigate possible causes for the behavioral, social, or learning challenges that you see in your child. This approach will be explained more in the following pages. Essentially, when one uses the problem-solving approach to understanding, information is gathered, and "working theories" are developed along the way that attempt to explain the behaviors of concern. These theories are modified as new information is obtained. Users of this approach continue to problem-solve and investigate until they are satisfied with the information they have obtained and the resulting level of understanding of the child.

Parents can easily adapt this problem-solving approach to use in their quest for understanding the needs of their child. Most parents do some sort of problem-solving when they are concerned about their children, but the problem-solving may not always be in an organized fashion. Also, parents may jump to early conclusions about their child's puzzling behavior because they are so eager to identify what is wrong with their child. Often, however, more investigation is actually needed to fully understand the child. For example, a child with little motivation to complete his school work may be seen as lazy and oppositional. Parents and teachers may prematurely conclude that the child needs some type of punishment when the school work is not completed. More careful investigation may reveal that the child has some type of learning difficulty that makes it incredibly hard for the child to keep up with the other children. In-depth investigation and problem-solving strategies can aid parents and teachers in finding the true source of the child's difficulties.

The Profile-Based Approach to Intervention

In *A Mind at a Time*, Mel Levine, MD stresses that "all kinds of people have all kinds of minds." He notes that people's minds are "wired" to do a variety of different tasks. Some people are "wired" to be engineers, and other people are "wired" to be actors. We are all different, and the world needs this diversity of talent in order to properly function. If we were all the same, our society would cease to operate.

Dr. Levine stresses that we can help all children become successful by better understanding their "neurodevelopmental profile." This profile consists of many systems, including the social thinking, attention-control, memory, higher thinking, motor, sequential ordering, spatial ordering, and language systems. These work together to form our minds. We need to identify the children's strengths and weaknesses in each of these areas in order to begin to "cultivate their minds" (i.e., addressing the weaknesses and building up the strengths).

I embrace Dr. Levine's concept of neurodevelopmental profiles and utilize this profile-based approach to intervention in my practice. When data is gathered during assessment activities, it is important to gather information about the strengths of the child. Strengths can include such talents as being able to build, having a high level of vocabulary, being able to draw, and having unique musical ability. Oftentimes in schools, the children with puzzling behavior are only reinforced when they demonstrate certain skills (e.g., reading, writing, sharing in groups). Other skills do not get reinforced as often (e.g., being able to design a building). Since we are all "wired" differently, the child with the natural proclivity to do well in reading and writing excels in school. The child with the natural proclivity to be nonverbal and build may be deemed as "odd" and not do as well on language-based tasks.

A profile can be made for a child once sufficient data is obtained about the areas of strength as well as those needing more growth. For example, a child may be very good at social conversation but have great difficulty conducting math calculations. This profile is just a description of the child's natural proclivities and learning thus far.

Once a profile is established, this information can be used for intervention planning. This profile is combined with the theory generated through the problem-solving mentioned earlier, in order to obtain a holistic view of the child. Interventions can then be designed based on this information. Interventions for the weak areas can be conducted using traditional intervention methods from such fields as special education, clinical psychology, speech/language pathology, or occupational therapy. However, interventions for areas of strength can be implemented using information from such fields as the booming area of "positive psychology" and other methods that are shown to improve that particular skill. Positive psychology, as described by Martin Seligman,[5] PhD, in his book *Authentic Happiness*, is an approach to behavioral difficulties that focuses on what we can do to make ourselves happier and function better. This is considerably different than the more traditional approach of targeting interventions only to reduce the problem behavior.

As noted above, I frequently utilize a strength-based approach in my practice. For example, I recently worked with a 9-year-old boy who demonstrated much anger in the classroom. He would not follow directions from the teacher, tore up his work, and walked around with a scowl on his face. In previous years, I would have primarily worked with the teachers to set up some type of behavior management system. Instead, I recommended that he receive supplemental instruction in writing to build on his strength in this area. With only a few tutoring sessions, his anger decreased, and he was much more appropriate. When you help a child become really good at something, it helps increase the child's confidence and self-esteem. This in turn helps the child become much more positive in interactions with others.

---

[5] Seligman, M. E. (2002). *Authentic happiness*. New York: Harper Collins.

CHAPTER THREE

Five Specific Steps to Finding the Right Solution

The actions that will lead to a comprehensive understanding and effective intervention for your child with behavioral, social, or learning challenges can be stated in five major steps:

1. Clarification of Concerns;
2. Functional Behavioral Assessment;
3. Investigation of Causal Factors;
4. Profile Development and Planning; and
5. Plan Implementation and Evaluation.

Each of these steps is fully described in the following pages and summary of is listed in Table 1: "Steps to Understanding and Intervention." Prior to implementing these steps, you are encouraged to consider the following two key points.

Think About Your Child in a Holistic Manner

One of the first things to think about when you or others have concerns about your child's puzzling behavior is to realize that behavior in general is multifaceted. Thus, the child with challenges may be even more arduous to understand. Since the difficulties are complex, it is important to look comprehensively at your child in a holistic manner. We have trouble even predicting certain simple behavior (e.g., when you will take two steps to the right), let alone predicting and figuring out complex behavioral, social, or learning challenges. Thus, it is important to look at all aspects of the child. Children demonstrate puzzling behavior for a number of reasons. Some of these reasons were discussed above. Other possible reasons include confusion with an assignment at school, conflict with a classmate, inadequate nutrition, poor sleep, boredom, inability to sit still for long periods of time, or behavior that has never been confronted by the child's parents. There are so many reasons for puzzling behavior that it is even difficult for seasoned professionals to figure children out and understand their behavior.

Be Wary of Quick Answers and Quick Fixes

In their desperation to find answers, parents and teachers will often gravitate to the professionals who give them a very simple and clear explanation for why a child may be having a particular problem. "Your child has ADHD." "Your child has Sensory Processing Disorder." "Your child has a cognitive processing disorder that makes it very difficult for him to attend." Parents also gravitate to professionals who give them very simple solutions for the child's behavioral issues. "Your child needs to be placed on medication right away." "Your child needs two days of speech/language therapy each week." "You just need to read this book, and it will help you fix everything."

The problem with accepting quick solutions and quick interventions is that many times, the parents and teachers find that these quick fixes are not the answer. Also, the cookbook approach does not work. After spending much money and time, parents find themselves back to square one, trying to figure out their child. Of course, there are times when there is a simple solution. Consider the following example. Recently, I worked with a young teenage boy with disruptive behavior. He had just moved out West from a major city on the East coast. His parents had divorced, and he was now coming to live with his father. After weeks of counseling related to his disruptive behavior, he spontaneously stated one day that he could not find his glasses. His father was astounded because he did not even know that his son wore glasses. Much of the disruptive behavior was due to the boy not being able to see!

Other simple solutions include (1) the child with an undiagnosed legitimate medical problem that can be easily treated, (2) the bright child who is bored and acts out until more challenging academic material is presented, and (3) an inattentive child who responds beautifully to stimulant medication, with no need for further intervention.

However, based on my experiences, the quest for a simple solution usually ends in disappointment. Many parents of children with special needs will tell you that it is extremely important for you to look and intervene with your child in a multifaceted and holistic fashion. Parents need to be cautious in quickly accepting that their child's puzzling behavior is due to a particular disorder, such as ADHD, Sensory Processing Disorder, Asperger's Disorder, or another type of disorder. Teachers and parents also need to be cautious and not quickly accept simple solutions. A child may have ADHD, or a child may have a true behavior disorder (e.g., Conduct Disorder), but a comprehensive look at the child must be conducted first before such a determination is made. Kids with anxiety often look like kids with ADHD. This is because their feelings of nervousness are manifested in hyperactive behavior since these children have difficulty expressing their feelings directly. An extreme example would be kids with brain tumors who can demonstrate learning deficits. A holistic and comprehensive look at the child will reveal an understanding that will help caregivers take more appropriate actions over the long term.

TABLE 1: STEPS TO UNDERSTANDING AND INTERVENTION

STEP	QUESTIONS TO CONSIDER	PROFESSIONAL TO CONSULT	ACTION STEPS
1. Clarification of Concerns	What are the specific behaviors of concern? When, where, and how often are the behaviors demonstrated?	Psychologist	Problem Worksheet Activities 1, 2, and 3
2. Functional Behavior Assessment (FBA)	What happens before and after the behaviors? What have the behaviors looked like over time? What stressors have had an impact on the behaviors?	Psychologist	ABC Worksheet Time Line/Stressor Worksheet Theory Building Worksheet Activities 4, 5, 6, and 7
3. Investigation of Causal Factors			
a. Medical/Developmental	Are there any undiagnosed medical or developmental difficulties?	Pediatrician/Family Practice Physician Developmental Pediatrician Other Medical Specialist	Causal Factors Worksheet Activity 8
b. Hearing/Vision	Are there any vision or hearing difficulties?	Optometrist or Audiologist	
c. Speech/Language	Are there any speech or language delays? Are there any difficulties with social interaction, communication, or play?	Speech/Language Pathologist	
d. Sensory/Motor	Are there any sensory, fine, or gross motor difficulties?	Occupational Therapist Physical Therapist	
e. Academic/Life Skills	Are there any delays in reading, math, or written language?	School Psychologist General or Special Education Teacher	

STEP	QUESTIONS TO CONSIDER	PROFESSIONAL TO CONSULT	ACTION STEPS
f. Cognitive/Neuro-psychological	Are there any suspected cognitive neuropsychological delays?	Clinical Psychologist Neuropsychologist	Causal Factors Worksheet Activity 8
g. Emotional/Psychiatric	Are there any emotional or psychiatric difficulties?	Clinical Psychologist Licensed Counselor Psychiatrist	
h. Other contributing causes: consider effects of classroom environment, culture, second language acquisition, family, religion, sexual orientation, and other factors known to affect behavior and learning	What is the child's cultural background? Is the child's language background other than English? What is the family composition? Are there any particular family difficulties? What is the family's religious background? Are there any concerns regarding the child's sexual orientation? Are there other factors, that could contribute to the child's difficulties? Based on the above information, what can you say about the child's behavior? Is the behavior abnormal? What factors contribute to the behavior? What is the child's profile of strengths and weaknesses? What are specific goals for the child? What are some intervention strategies?	Psychologist or other Mental Health Professional	
4. Profile Development and Planning	How is my child responding to the intervention?	Any of the professionals listed above	Theory Building Worksheet Intervention
5. Plan Implementation and Evaluation	Are there any adjustments that need to be made?	Any of the professionals listed above	Review of Intervention Planning Worksheet Activity 11

Download reproducible worksheets at www.lifespanpress.com. Activities are located in Chapter Three. A sample scenario and examples of completed forms may be found beginning on page 70.

Step #1: Clarification of Concerns

If you are a parent of a child with puzzling behavior, ask yourself the following questions: Am I clear on what my and others' concerns are? Can I state these concerns in specific terms? How many specific concerns do I have? The reason you ask these questions is that often people think initially that they know what their concerns are. However, upon closer examination, they often are actually a bit confused about the specific nature of the concerns.

It is a valuable exercise to list all of your concerns on a piece a paper, make the concerns as specific as possible, and then prioritize them in terms of what behavior is most troubling. Activity #1 helps to guide you through this process. When concerns are clarified, it becomes much easier to design an intervention plan. For example, suppose you have a child in the fourth grade that is suspected of having an attention disorder. Let's say the teachers complain that he cannot pay attention. They also complain that he is disruptive and does not want to do his work. What are the specific concerns in this scenario? To clarify them, you would need to know exactly what the teachers mean by "attention problems." Having attention problems could mean that he has trouble paying attention when the teacher is reading a book. It could also mean that he has trouble staying focused in written language activities. "Attention problems" could mean lots of things. Clarifying what "it" means for him will help narrow down where exactly the problems lie.

ACTIVITY #1: LISTING CONCERNS IN SPECIFIC AND MEASURABLE TERMS

As noted above, when trying to understand and intervene with your child's puzzling behavior, the first task you need to do is write down all the concerns that you and others have. Take out a blank piece of paper, and write down all the concerns that you have about your child. When listing concerns, place them in bullet point form, and be as specific as you can. For example, if you are worried about your child's self-esteem, what exactly do you mean? What is self-esteem to you? Do you think your child has negative self-esteem because of his/her statements about him/herself? Is it because he/she is not speaking up in a group? After you have listed the concerns, do your best to group the common ones together. For example, irritable behavior and angry outbursts can go together. Poor social skills and not being able to work cooperatively with others may go together. When behaviors are appropriately grouped together, a more comprehensive view of the child can be developed.

ACTIVITY #2: PRIORITIZING BEHAVIORS

Next, ask yourself some questions. Which behaviors are of most concern? Which behaviors are of least concern? It is very difficult for anyone to change their entire personality and behavior repertoire. It is much more effective to focus on changing one or two behaviors rather than trying to fix everything at once. Pinpoint the three behaviors of most concern. Write these behaviors on the Problem Worksheet located on the next page. Then, be as specific as you can regarding what each behavior looks like, how often it occurs, where it happens, and its duration. You can be very specific in this section since behavior is multidimensional. A sample scenario and examples of completed forms may be found beginning on page 70.

ACTIVITY #3: NATURALISTIC OBSERVATIONS

This activity can be completed either prior to Activity #1 or after Activity #2. The task is to complete a "naturalistic observation" of your child. Naturalistic observation is the method that many psychologists and anthropologists initially use to study a particular population of individuals. This type of observation is very helpful in clarifying the

PROBLEM WORKSHEET

CHILD'S NAME _____

In the "Behavior of Concern" column, list specific behaviors of concern. For example, "hits sister." Under the column "Specifics," note when this behavior occurs, where this behavior occurs, and how oftern this behavior occurs. Put a star by the behavior that you are most concerned about. Under "Comments or Insights," list what additional comments or insights you may have had.

BEHAVIOR OF CONCERN (e.g., hitting)	SPECIFICS (e.g., when, where, how often does the behavior occur)
1.	
2.	
3.	
4.	
5.	

COMMENTS OR INSIGHTS:

Download reproducible worksheets at www.lifespanpress.com.

behaviors of concern, prioritizing behaviors of concern, and understanding the causal factors related to the behaviors of concern.

To conduct the naturalistic observation, follow these steps: (1) Think of the time period when your child demonstrates the puzzling behavior most, (2) Observe your child during that time period, and (3) Write down observations on a blank piece of paper. Be in the environment, but try to stay disengaged. You are the observer, and you are to observe the behavior without any judgments, interpretations, interferences, or preconceived notions. Decide how much time you want to observe, and stick to this time frame. As you observe, write down everything you see or hear. You will be writing very quickly, so write in shorthand or whatever method you can use to capture everything you see. Try to observe without any judgments. For example, rather than stating, "George is happy," write down, "George is smiling and is talking to his sister." Once you are done with this observation, you can do other observations in other environments and situations. Of course, the more observations the better, but it is not always practical to do more than one to three observations.

When you have completed your observations, go back over your notes. Respond to the following questions: What types of behaviors do you see? What types of patterns do you see? Do you have any particular insights? What behaviors seem to be of most concern? If you have done Activities #1 and #2 first, go back through the results of these activities to determine if any adjustments to your concerns are needed.

As mentioned at the beginning of this exercise, naturalistic observation is extremely effective in helping to identify and clarify puzzling behavior. It sounds very simplistic, but it is not. Researchers have documented for years that our perceptions as human beings are not always accurate. We may think we are seeing a particular phenomenon accurately, but this is not always the case. By being objective in your observations, you may find yourself seeing behaviors or events that you have not seen before now. You will open up your mind and be able to see patterns that you did not know existed.

Step #2: Functional Behavioral Assessment

Functional behavioral assessment (FBA) is a systematic way of gathering information in order to determine a relationship between a child's behavior of concern and aspects of the environment. FBA is most commonly used by school professionals, including special education teachers, school psychologists, and school counselors. The purpose of the FBA is to help understand why a child engages in puzzling behavior, when/where the puzzling behavior is most likely to occur, and under what conditions the child will be most successful. This information helps observers to formulate hypotheses (summary statements), in order to guide the development of effective behavior intervention plans.

FBAs are based on several assumptions. The first assumption is that all behavior is supported by current environmental conditions. For example, attention difficulties may be influenced by the teacher inadequately giving positive feedback to the child. The second assumption is that all behavior serves a function (e.g., to obtain something positive, to escape, to reduce certain sensory experiences); for example, angry outbursts could be due to the child not wanting anyone to get emotionally close. The third assumption is that puzzling behavior can be changed through the use of positive intervention strategies. This means that behavior can be changed regardless of the causal factors behind the behavior; for example, even though some childhood depression has been shown to be genetically based, it is still possible to increase the child's happiness through certain therapeutic strategies.

STEPS OF THE FBA

The process of the FBA involves the following distinct steps:

Step #1: Determine the priority of the behavior of concern. In this step, the person conducting the assessment must decide if the behavior of concern is of high priority to be changed. Sometimes certain behaviors are annoying but not severe enough to warrant specialized assessment and intervention. Thus, a conscious decision must be made – change the behavior of concern or let the behavior remain as it is and put up with any annoyances that it may cause. In Activity #2, behaviors of concern were prioritized, and these will now become the focus for the FBA, as you will note below.

Step #2: Select and define target behaviors. The second step of the FBA is to select and define one or several target behaviors. A "target behavior" is the behavior that you will attempt to change. Children with puzzling behavior often present with many behaviors of concern. It is difficult to address all the problem behaviors, and it is much more effective, and recommended, to concentrate on only one or two concerns at a time. Part of this selection of target behaviors is to make sure they are well-defined, in order to facilitate the most effective interventions.

Step #3: Identify the function of the puzzling behavior using "ABCs." The third step of FBA is to identify the possible function of the behavior of concern. In many cases, the function of the behavior is clear. The word "function" is used to indicate "what is the reason" for the child demonstrating the behavior. Sometimes, the function of the behavior is not clear, and more systematic observation is required.

In order to identify the function of the behavior, it is necessary to identify the setting events, antecedents, and consequences related to the target behavior in question. Setting events are the more "distant" events that happen at some point prior to the demonstrated target behavior. Examples of setting events include having a pre-existing condition of Attention-Deficit/Hyperactivity Disorder (ADHD), having parents who are in conflict, or struggling with a fluctuating mood disorder. Setting events can also be concurrent events, such as hunger, pain, or fatigue. Antecedents are the "proximal" events that immediately precede the target behaviors of concern. Setting events are often seen as setting the stage for the target behavior to occur, and the antecedent events are the events that actually trigger the behavior to occur. Consequences are those events that occur after the demonstration of the target behavior. In the example of scolding a child for a tantrum, "scolding" is considered the consequence.

Oftentimes, psychologists analyze the "ABCs" of behavior. This means that the psychologist analyzes the antecedents ("A") and consequences ("C") in relation to the target behavior ("B"). When the setting events and the ABCs are analyzed, we often gain a clearer idea of why the puzzling behavior is occurring. The function of the behavior then is more easily identified. In this step, the person conducting the assessment analyzes the data and formulates hypotheses regarding the function of the behavior. For instance, an aggressive outburst could function as a means to avoid a particularly challenging activity.

Step #4: Formulate summary statements. The fourth step of FBA is to formulate "summary statements" related to the problem behavior and the previous analyses. Once the concerns are clarified and the behaviors of concern are analyzed according to the "ABCs," it is then necessary to put this information together into a form called "summary statements." Summary statements describe what is happening with a particular behavior and what the function of the particular behavior seems to be. The "function" of the behavior could be a number of factors, such as to avoid something that is perceived as negative, gain attention, reduce overstimulation, or prevent someone else from doing something. Summary statements capture all the given information into one or two sentences.

The form of the summary statements is as follows: Given a particular situation (setting event), when "A" happens (antecedent), the person will demonstrate "B," and typically "C" occurs. It appears that the function of the behavior is to . . . (state a reason). Suppose you have a child who does not like school work:

Sonya does not like to do any type of reading or written material. When she is presented with any type of work, she can become very disruptive. The teacher often becomes very frustrated and then sends her to the principal's office. Upon close analysis, sending Sonya to the principal's office actually seems to increase her disruption in the classroom.

Based on this information, a summary statement could be as follows:

Given that Sonya has reading difficulties, when Sonya is presented with academic material she has to read, she often becomes disruptive. The teacher first reprimands her and oftentimes sends her to the principal's office. It appears that the function of Sonya's behavior is to escape from having to do her school work.

This is a very common scenario that teachers and parents overlook. Kids can become nervous, fidgety, or oppositional because they may not want to do something or because they find the work challenging. Instead of buckling down and focusing, they may instead become disruptive and then be pleased when they are finally asked to leave.

Summary statements are the beginnings of the theory that you are developing about why your child is demonstrating particular puzzling behavior. A "theory" is what you have proposed to be the reason for the occurrence of the behavior. As you go through the remainder of this guide, your original theory may change or at least be modified. Suppose your summary statements sound like this:

When Milando's routine has been disrupted, (e.g., when he is presented with after-school homework), he will begin yelling and screaming that he does not want to do it. We, the parents, back off and let him play instead. The function of his tantrum-like behavior appears to be to help him avoid doing the particular activity.

Now, suppose you also discover later that your child seems to have fine-motor difficulties. Your "theory" as to why your child is oppositional at times could be as follows:

> Milando appears to demonstrate tantrums to get out of doing tasks that he does not like doing. Some of the reasons that he does not like doing the tasks are that he has great difficulty doing any type of fine motor work. Rather than persist in working through his difficulties, he has learned to become disruptive instead.

What you have created is a working theory on which you can base your intervention. The process of "ruling out" or investigating other factors and intervention planning is discussed below.

One word of note: In the schools, completion of FBAs is common since certain federal laws require that students with disabilities who demonstrate behavioral challenges must have been evaluated using an FBA before any changes of placement or school suspension lasting longer than 10 days. Thus, FBAs in the schools may be thought of as just a legal requirement. However, this is false. The techniques represent an approach that helps systematically analyze the conditions surrounding behaviors of concern. Thus, the FBA is not merely a form or a hoop to jump. The FBA is a tool for others to use to collect quality data so that effective interventions can be better designed and implemented. Creating an FBA for your child, based on your observations as a parent, generates a powerful and effective tool for intervening on behalf of your child.

Another word of note: There are professionals who do not believe in evaluating children using the FBA, since other factors (e.g., assessment of the child's ability to self-regulate) are seen as the core of the puzzling behavior in children. I understand why these clinicians are skeptical of the FBA; much behavior may not always be due primarily to environmental conditions. For example, more often than not, challenges in social interaction for a child with Autistic Disorder are not due to environmental events or lack of teaching. Instead, these challenges are due to something inherent in the child's physiological state. I agree with these clinicians in that much puzzling behavior is due to the internal makeup of the child. However, the FBA can still be a very useful tool. I have used it many times successfully in my practice. Parents throughout time have used this approach in some form or another. In my mind, the FBA can be used with almost any theoretical approach. All we are doing with the FBA in this guide is clarifying what the concerns are, collecting some data, and forming initial hypotheses. I am not preaching that all behavior is learned or that all behavior is due to some type of environmental event. I believe that puzzling behavior is too complex to make such simplistic statements. The use of the FBA is only a starting point. Later, as additional reasons for the puzzling behavior are discovered, this new information can then be woven into these initial hypotheses so that a comprehensive understanding of the child can be achieved. When clinicians do not use an objective process, such as the FBA, to initially evaluate a child, I believe these clinicians jump to conclusions too quickly regarding why a child has puzzling behavior. This can lead to false conclusions, which can be quite damaging to the child and family.

The completion of the FBA may sound complex, but in actuality it is not. In the following activities, the reader will be guided through the process of an FBA.[6] Activities #1, #2, and #3 help provide initial data for the FBA. Activities #4, #5, #6, and #7 complete the process.

---

[6] For further reading about functional behavioral assessment, the reader is directed to the following resource: Chandler, L. K., & Dahlquist, C. M. (2005). *Functional assessment: Strategies to prevent and remediate challenging behavior in school settings.* Columbus: Merrill Prentice Hall.

ACTIVITY #4: ANTECEDENTS, BEHAVIORS, AND CONSEQUENCES

In this activity, parents are asked to analyze the "antecedents" and "consequences" of a particular behavior of concern. All this really means is that we want to determine what event comes immediately before the behavior (the antecedent) and what event comes immediately after the behavior (the consequence). For example, suppose a middle school student hits another student. The hitting is the "B," or behavior. What could possibly come before the hitting? The student could have been teased about something. Thus, the antecedent, or "A," is teasing. What could possibly come after the hitting? Perhaps the student being hit becomes so scared of the student that he stops the teasing. In this case, the consequence, or "C," is fear in the student being hit. "Consequence" in this case only refers to an event that comes immediately after the behavior, and it does not refer to a punishment. The "ABCs" of this behavior are the following:

A	B	C
Teasing	Hitting	Fear—results in teaser stopping the teasing.

Looking at the ABCs of the behavior is extremely important in the understanding of puzzling behavior because puzzling behavior is often caused by some environmental stimuli or is strengthened by some event that occurs after it.

Locate the ABCs Worksheet on the next page. On this worksheet, list the behaviors of concern in the behavior column. Then, through observations, interviewing of others, or from your own knowledge base, note what typically comes immediately before the behavior and what comes immediately afterward. Also, in the "Setting Event" column, note situations or conditions that increase the likelihood that a particular behavior may occur. For example, people tend to get

ABCs WORKSHEET

CHILD'S NAME _____

Step 1: List behavior of concern in three words or less in "B." Step 2: List factors in "Setting Event" that contribute long term to the behavior of concern (e.g., school failure, family arguing, etc.). Step 3: List in "A" events that come immediately before the behavior of concern (e.g., directions given). Step 4: List in "C" what happens immediately after the behavior. Once these steps are completed, look for patterns and potential points for intervention and note under "Comments or Insights."

SETTING EVENT	ANTECEDENT "A"	BEHAVIOR "B"	CONSEQUENCES "C"
		1.	
		2.	
		3.	

COMMENTS OR INSIGHTS:

Download reproducible worksheets at www.lifespanpress.com.

angry more easily when they are stressed or tired. With your child, is it possible that the behavior is demonstrated more frequently when people are over to visit, or after a long day at school, or when plans have changed? There are a number of possibilities, but try to identify those times when the behavior is most likely to occur. Once you have done this, note any patterns that you see. Be as objective as you can. A sample scenario and examples of completed forms may be found beginning on page 70.

ACTIVITY #5: PROBLEM AND SCHEDULE TRACKING SHEETS

Another way to analyze the behavior of concern is to note how often and for how long the behavior occurs. An easy way to note this information is to use the Problem Tracking Sheet located on the next page. For each behavior of concern, record on the tracking sheet the day and time the behavior occurs. For instance, a child with frequent temper tantrums may be noted to demonstrate these tantrums on Monday through Friday at 9 am. Also, many behaviors may be extended in length. This can be noted on the tracking sheet as well. For example, a tantrum from the above child may last anywhere from 10 minutes to more than 30 minutes. Thus, on Mondays and Wednesdays, tantrums last from about 9 am until 9:10 am. However, on Tuesdays, Thursdays, and Fridays, the tantrums may last an average of 45 minutes. For example, the tantrums may last from 9 am until 9:45 am. Oftentimes, problem behaviors are only demonstrated at certain times of the day or in certain settings. By plotting the behavior on a schedule, you can see when the behavior is demonstrated, and then interventions can be designed to prevent the behavior from occurring. Most explosive behavior is predictable when tracked and analyzed in this manner.

Along with noting the behaviors on the problem tracking sheet, it is often helpful to note the child's typical schedule on the Schedule Tracking Sheet, located on the next page. For example, a child may

PROBLEM TRACKING SHEET

CHILD'S NAME _____

Fill in this form by noting when the problem behavior of concern is typically demonstrated.

	SUNDAY	MONDAY	TUESDAY	WEDNESDAY	THURSDAY	FRIDAY	SATURDAY
Dates:							
Morning							
6:00							
6:30							
7:00							
7:30							
8:00							
8:30							
9:00							
9:30							
10:00							
10:30							
11:00							
11:30							
Afternoon							
12:00							
12:30							
1:00							
1:30							
2:00							
2:30							
3:00							
3:30							
4:00							
4:30							
5:00							
5:30							
Evening							
6:00							
6:30							
7:00							
7:30							
8:00							
8:30							
9:00							
9:30							
10:00							
10:30							
11:00							
Night							
12:00							
1:00							
2:00							
3:00							
4:00							
5:00							
5:30							

COMMENTS:

Download reproducible worksheets at www.lifespanpress.com.

CHILD'S TYPICAL SCHEDULE

CHILD'S NAME _____

Fill in this form as completely as possible with your child's typical schedule.

	SUNDAY	MONDAY	TUESDAY	WEDNESDAY	THURSDAY	FRIDAY	SATURDAY
Dates:							
Morning							
6:00							
6:30							
7:00							
7:30							
8:00							
8:30							
9:00							
9:30							
10:00							
10:30							
11:00							
11:30							
Afternoon							
12:00							
12:30							
1:00							
1:30							
2:00							
2:30							
3:00							
3:30							
4:00							
4:30							
5:00							
5:30							
Evening							
6:00							
6:30							
7:00							
7:30							
8:00							
8:30							
9:00							
9:30							
10:00							
10:30							
11:00							
Night							
12:00							
1:00							
2:00							
3:00							
4:00							
5:00							
5:30							

COMMENTS:

Download reproducible worksheets at www.lifespanpress.com.

rise at 6:30 am, eat at 6:45 am, go to school at 8 am, etc. Once the schedule is listed on the schedule tracking sheet, data from this sheet can be compared to the data on the problem tracking sheet. What is noted many times is that certain behaviors occur at certain times of the day in response to some type of event in the schedule. A sample scenario and examples of completed forms may be found beginning on page 70.

ACTIVITY #6: TIMELINE AND STRESSORS

Puzzling behavior can take many forms. Some types of puzzling behavior are noticeable early on in the child's life. Other puzzling behavior develops during some particular time period. When trying to understand puzzling behavior, it is important to analyze not only the events currently influencing the behavior, but also the course of the behavior over time. It is also important to look at what major "stressors" in the child's life could have contributed to the development of the behavior of concern. Stressors are those life events that could have an impact on a person's emotional and behavioral status. For instance, the changing of schools is a stressor. Having a parent change a job is another stressor. Making a visual representation of the behavior over time and identifying the stressors in the child's life may shed some light on the child's behavior.

This activity is meant to help you develop a timeline for your child's puzzling behavior and to identify stressors that could have impacted the puzzling behavior. Locate the Timeline/Stressor Worksheet on the following page. Pick a behavior of concern, and try to note on this worksheet when the behavior was first observed. Rate this behavior on a scale from 1 (not severe) to 10 (very severe). Next, go through each year of the child's life, and rate how the behavior was for that year, trying to be as objective as possible. Next, on the timeline, list any particular stressors that happened during that particular year in the space

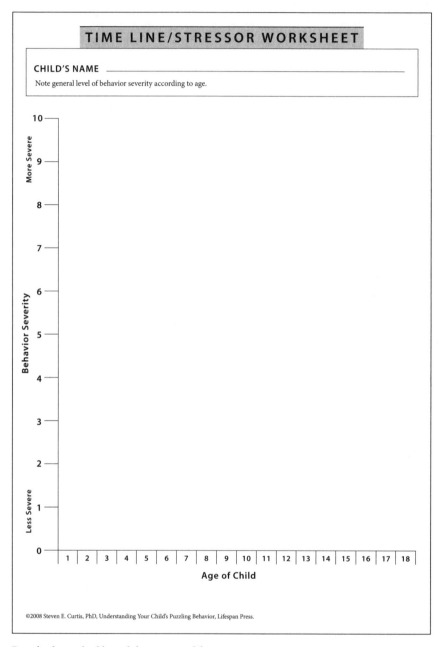

TIME LINE/STRESSOR WORKSHEET

CHILD'S NAME _____

Note general level of behavior severity according to age.

Download reproducible worksheets at www.lifespanpress.com.

next to the corresponding year. Did you move? Did your child lose a pet? Did your child have trouble in school?

After you have completed the timeline and have identified stressors, take a look at your material, and see if you notice any trends. This can be a very effective way to understand difficulties. For instance, suppose you have a high school student who has become very withdrawn and does not want to do any school work. A timeline will help you understand the events that led up to his poor motivation. In this case, the young man experienced learning difficulties back in the fourth grade. He felt dumb at that time but still kept a good attitude. As he progressed through the grades, his attitude toward school became increasingly negative. Teachers and his parents began lecturing him and telling him stuff like, "You have to learn this to get a job." He began to tune them out, and he became very good at doing so. Finally, in high school, his immediate reaction to all school work was to "check out" and ignore others around him. By reviewing this timeline with him, along with the stressors he experienced at certain times, we were able to help him and his parents understand why he was demonstrating his current behavior. This helped him tremendously, and now he is completing significantly more school work than he has done in the past.

ACTIVITY #7: PUTTING IT ALL TOGETHER INTO SUMMARY STATEMENTS

In this activity, your task is to generate summary statements for each behavior of concern. Locate the Theory Building Worksheet on page 60. The summary statements from this activity will be placed on that worksheet. The first step is to review the information you obtained on your child in the previous activities. The second step is to fill in the information as noted below:

1. Pick a behavior of concern on which to complete a summary statement.

2. What are some overall conditions that could be considered setting events? Remember, setting events are events that make the behavior of concern more likely to occur. For example, are there any particular stressors, such as family conflict? When you decide on the setting event, begin a sentence as follows:

   a. Given that [setting event] . . .

3. Next, list the identified "antecedent" and place it in the sentence. Remember, this is the event that has been determined to precede the behavior of concern. Complete the following part of this sentence:

   a. Given that [setting event], when [antecedent] . . .

4. In this part, list what your child does. Be specific, and complete this part of the sentence:

   a. Given that [setting event], when [antecedent], [name of your child] will [list the behavior of concern in specific terms] . . .

5. To complete the summary statement, describe the "consequence" or what comes after the behavior. You can put this as a completion of the previous sentence, or you can make a new sentence.

   a. Given that [setting event], when [antecedent], [name of your child] will [list the behavior of concern in specific terms]. . . . Oftentimes, after [name of your child] demonstrates this behavior, [describe what comes after the behavior, i.e., the "consequence"].

6. The final part of the summary statement has to do with describing the function of the behavior. This is best stated as a separate sentence, as follows:

   a. First list your completed summary statement as noted in #5 above. Then state: Thus, the function of the behavior appears to be [describe the function of the behavior].

It is recommended that you complete summary statements for each behavior of concern. Sometimes you can actually combine the summary statements together to make a comprehensive statement. As discussed before, these statements provide the foundation for your theory as to why a child is demonstrating a particular puzzling behavior. Summary statements alone can be very therapeutic, in that parents often have insights as to how to best meet the current needs of their children.

A sample scenario and examples of completed forms may be found beginning on page 70.

Step #3: Investigating Other Factors

By the time you reach this step, you should have gathered the following information. First, you should have identified the behaviors of most concern and analyzed these behaviors with a number of tools. You should have attempted to locate the function of the behavior and formulated summary statements pertaining to the behaviors of concern. With simple behavioral issues, this may be all you need to do in order to best understand and intervene with your child's puzzling behavior. If, for example, you discovered that your child demonstrates tantrums every day at 4 pm, and the tantrums seem to be related to being hungry, you have found exactly what you need to do. You need to feed your child! If this is the case, you can go straight to intervention planning, and skip this next step.

However, in most cases, puzzling behavior is not always that easy to understand. The FBA helps you to develop an initial theory for why your child demonstrates puzzling behavior. But oftentimes you need to gather more information. On most occasions, you need to "rule out" other possible causes. The term "rule out" is a term psychologists and other healthcare professionals use to refer to investigating other alternative explanations.

There are many potential reasons for why your child is demonstrating the puzzling behavior of concern. The following sections outline possible causes.

MEDICAL OR DEVELOPMENTAL

Children with puzzling behavior could have some type of undiagnosed medical difficulty. By medical difficulties, I am referring to concerns other than those typically in the realm of psychiatric difficulties, such as an attention disorder, mood disorder, or anxiety disorder. These difficulties are usually ruled out by such professionals as family practice physicians and pediatricians. For more complicated developmental issues, children are referred for evaluation by developmental pediatricians, who are specialists in both pediatric medicine and developmental disorders.[7]

HEARING AND VISION

Children with puzzling behavior may be demonstrating this behavior because of vision or hearing difficulties. Hearing difficulties can take many forms. Children can have deficits in the hearing of sounds. Children can also have deficits in the hearing or processing of sounds in noisy environments. Classrooms are sometimes noisy, and children with difficulties discriminating auditory information may demonstrate inattentive behavior because they have trouble hearing. Vision difficulties can also take many forms, including simple vision problems to more serious difficulties (e.g., being able to effectively keep his eyes on the print [i.e., visual tracking]). The child's vision and hearing should be evaluated by qualified optometrists (or an ophthalmologist) and audiologists.

---

[7] For a fascinating review of this area, the reader is encouraged to read the following resource: Eide, B., & Eide, F. (2007). *The mislabeled child*. New York: Hyperion Press.

SPEECH, LANGUAGE, AND SOCIAL FACTORS

At times, puzzling behavior can be explained by difficulties with speech or language. Speech and language difficulties can take many forms, from the more simple speech difficulties to the more complex application of social language, called "pragmatics." Some children may appear to have a good understanding of vocabulary or sentence structure but may be unable to use their language effectively in a social context. Language difficulties can be one reason for social skills deficits and difficulties with peer relationships. The evaluation of language skills is a complex process and should be conducted only by qualified speech/language pathologists.

SENSORY AND MOTOR FACTORS

The ability to use the large muscles in activities such as running, and the ability to use the smaller muscles in activities such as writing, can have a great impact on the emotional well-being and performance of a child. In addition, sensory difficulties can greatly impact how a child functions on a daily basis.

Some children are found to have what is known as "Sensory Processing Disorder" (SPD). SPD is considered to be a neurological disorder, first described 40 years ago by Jean Ayres, PhD, OTR (Occupational Therapist Registered). Dr. Ayres developed a sensory processing theory to explain the relationship between behavior and brain functioning. She noted that much sensory information enters our brain at any given moment from our eyes, ears, and every other place on our bodies. The brain must integrate all of these sensations in order to create normal learning and movement. How we process these stimuli has a major impact on our feelings, thoughts, and actions. When we have problems with sensory processing, there are often confusing behaviors which occur, such as extreme fear or avoidance, or conversely, constant seeking of particular sensory experiences. Examples of behaviors associated with SPD in children include: (1) inability to filter out background noise, (2) low/floppy muscle tone, (3) hand flapping, and (4) sensitivity to tight or stiff clothing. Fine motor skills and sensory processing are specialty areas of many occupational therapists.

When a child presents with puzzling behavior, it is a good idea to have the child evaluated by an occupational or physical therapist, depending on the presenting difficulty. Occupational therapists traditionally focus on helping children with fine motor, sensory, and life-skill types of intervention. Physical therapists focus on interventions with large muscles and other aspects of the human body. However, today the two professions often overlap in their service pattern. Thus, it is up to the individual provider to determine which aspects of the child will be evaluated.

ACADEMIC AND LIFE SKILLS

For most children, school is a major part of their day-to-day life. They are expected to attend, listen, work with others, and complete work as assigned. It is very common for puzzling behavior to be associated with academic skill deficits. Not being able to do the assigned work can be very frustrating. Frustration can lead to off-task and disruptive behavior. As a child matures, mastery of life skills is essential. Examples of life skills include telling time, tying one's shoes, eating food properly, counting money, and driving a car. The professionals who are experts in evaluating academic and life skills include general and special education teachers, school psychologists, and some educational consultants.

COGNITIVE AND NEUROPSYCHOLOGICAL SKILLS

Cognitive and neuropsychological skills refer to those brain-based abilities that are fundamental to learning. Examples of these skills include memory, problem solving, visual-motor, vocabulary knowledge, visual-spatial, and processing speed. Visual-motor skills are those skills that have to do with eye-hand coordination, such as using a pencil for written language. Visual-spatial skills are used when designing a building or building a tower with blocks. Processing speed refers to how quickly someone completes a particular task.

When a child has strengths or deficits in cognitive skills, this can affect learning. Memory deficits can make it hard to retain or recall information. Difficulty with visual-motor skills will make it difficult to learn to write. Being slow with processing will make it difficult to complete tasks in a timely manner. Having trouble with visual-spatial skills will make it difficult to draw or complete puzzles. Experts in this area include clinical psychologists and neuropsychologists. School psychologists are also well-trained to complete a limited number of tests in this area.

A common factor that is overlooked by clinicians and parents is in the area of giftedness. We all come into this world with a certain potential to learn. Some people are very challenged with learning activities of all kinds. Others find most learning easy. Then there are those individuals who have an extremely high level of cognitive talent, and these individuals may be found to be "gifted." Gifted children are often misdiagnosed as having attention problems or even Autistic Disorder. However, upon closer examination, these children may demonstrate behaviors that are typical of gifted children. Such children often look unusual since their minds may always be working at full speed, and their interests may be different from those of other children their same age.[8]

EMOTIONAL AND PSYCHIATRIC FACTORS

As you are learning, puzzling behavior can take many forms and have many possible causes. One of the common causes for puzzling behavior is the presence of some type of emotional or psychiatric disorder. Puzzling behavior can be caused by common emotional reactions

---

[8] For further reading in this area, the reader is encouraged to consult the following resource: Webb, J., Amend, E., Webb, N., Goerss, J., Beljan, P., & Olenchak, F. (2005). *Misdiagnosis and dual diagnosis of gifted children and adults*. Scottsdale, AZ: Great Potential Press.

resulting from such events as a death of a loved one or pet, frustration in school, or trouble with peer relationships. At other times, puzzling behavior can be caused by a more formal psychiatric disorder. Examples of childhood psychiatric disorders in children include Major Depressive Disorder, Generalized Anxiety Disorder, Attention-Deficit/ Hyperactivity Disorder (ADHD), and Autistic Disorder. Parents often jump to the conclusion that a psychiatric disorder is present before investigating the other factors above. Please remember not to jump to conclusions or to look for quick fixes. Instead, it is important to explore the presence of psychiatric disorders while at the same time investigating other possible contributing factors. Experts in this area include clinical psychologists, psychiatrists, psychiatric nurse practitioners, and licensed mental health counselors.

OTHER CONTRIBUTING CAUSES

There are many other possible causal factors that contribute to puzzling behavior. It is practically impossible to list all of them. Puzzling behavior can be associated with a challenging classroom environment, a student's ethnicity or culture, second language acquisition, family constellation, religious affiliation, and sexual orientation. Some of the questions to be asked include the following: Are the parents and teachers using effective management strategies at home and school? Is the curriculum at school engaging? Are there any concerns with the establishment of relationships? What is the child's ethnicity and cultural background? Is the child's language background something other than English? What is the family composition? Are there any particular family difficulties? What is the family's religious background? Are there any questions regarding the child's sexual orientation? Are there other factors that could contribute to the child's difficulties? Does the child watch too much TV or have too much screen time with the computer or video games?

ACTIVITY #8: CAUSAL FACTORS WORKSHEET

Locate the Causal Factors Worksheet on the next page. As you investigate causal factors related to your child's puzzling behavior, note information on this worksheet. There is no need to report extensive details. Instead, make simple notes that will help jog your memory as to what you have learned. By completing this worksheet, you will have a quick summary of what you have learned about your child. This will aid you in your theory development in the next chapter. A sample scenario and examples of completed forms may be found beginning on page 70.

Step #4: Profile Development and Planning

Gathering sufficient information to develop a comprehensive plan can be quite time consuming. However, I encourage parents never to stop looking for information to understand their child, since new information will most likely become available as time passes. This information may shed even more insight into what intervention strategies are needed. As any parent with a child with special needs knows, as the child matures, different issues surface. Thus, parents are constantly challenged with new issues to address. Sometimes issues are resolved quickly in the assessment process. At other times, more extensive intervention is warranted.

In this section, we will discuss some of the basic aspects of intervention planning. As noted in the Introduction, my approach to intervention is called the "profile-based approach," which is consistent with the approach advocated by Mel Levine, MD.[9] The steps of Dr. Levine's approach are as follows:

1. Develop neurodevelopmental profile;
2. Discuss demystification with child;
3. Make accommodations;
4. Strengthen the strengths;

[9] See reference in Chapter 5: Parent Resources on page 116.

CAUSAL FACTORS WORKSHEET

CHILD'S NAME _____

As you investigate possible causes for your child's puzzling behavior, list the information obtained on this sheet. By completing this form, you can have a quick overview of possible contributing causes. As you complete this sheet, note any insights.

POSSIBLE FACTOR	RESULT
Medical/Developmental	
Hearing/Vision	
Speech/Language	
Sensory/Motor	
Academic/Life Skills	
Cognitive/Neuropsychological	
Emotional	
Other Possible Factors	

COMMENTS OR INSIGHTS:

Download reproducible worksheets at www.lifespanpress.com.

5. Intervene at the breakdown points; and

6. Protect from humiliation.

Dr. Levine is a strong advocate for developing a neurodevelopmental profile of the child's strengths and weaknesses. By using observations, review of previous information, and more formalized evaluation procedures, Dr. Levine develops a profile describing what the child can easily do and with what the child struggles. Once the profile is developed, Dr. Levine discusses it with the child. This process is called "demystification," which serves to help the child understand his/her own individual strengths and weaknesses.

Dr. Levine uses his assessment data to complete the remaining four steps. "Make accommodations" refers to helping the child understand how to be successful in learning, despite having a particular weakness. For example, if a child has vision impairments, the child must learn to use auditory aids to help acquire the desired information. "Intervene at the breakdown points" describes when a teacher or parent intervenes at crucial times when the child is struggling. For example, some children have difficulty with sustained problem-solving. In this case, when a child is seen as struggling with a particular task, the teacher or parent will intervene directly by teaching the child a particular strategy to solve the task.

"Protect from humiliation" refers to helping the child to feel confident when taking risks. Dr. Levine points out that the taking of risks is extremely important in the learning process. When a child does not take risks, learning is hampered. Thus, it is important to create a safe environment so that the child feels comfortable taking risks and does not feel humiliated after doing so.

As noted, in my work with children, I incorporate Dr. Levine's philosophies in my profile-based approach to intervention. In this approach, parents are asked to develop a profile for their child and then design interventions in both the areas of strength and the areas of weakness. When a child receives interventions in both areas, self-esteem is increased, frustration is reduced, and more progress is noted with the areas of concern. Oftentimes, professionals and others only intervene in the areas of concern. Children thereby often begin to feel that something is horribly wrong with them, and they begin viewing themselves in a negative light. The next section highlights how a theory and a profile of a child are developed.

THEORY BUILDING

You have been instructed to investigate a number of possible causes for your child's puzzling behavior. You may have consulted with a number of professionals. You might have received a number of diverse opinions on why your child is demonstrating the puzzling behavior. In this step, parents are instructed to build a theory as to why the child is demonstrating the puzzling behavior of concern. This working theory will help in the development of an intervention plan.

In the Introduction, I described a child who was brought to the psychologist's office because people were concerned about his social behavior. Let's suppose the parent completed all the steps above and is now in the process of theory building. Based on a review of data, the parent developed the following theory:

> "In a new social setting, John often appears disinterested and aloof. He does not give eye contact and speaks softly. Others think he has Asperger's Disorder, but I have concluded that this is not the case because in other settings, John has many friendships and seems to enjoy his close relationships. I believe that John demonstrates these social difficulties because he becomes uncomfortable in new situations. He is very mechanically oriented and loves to build. Both of his parents are engineers. He likes to talk about technical things. When others are "chatting," he withdraws because he does not like this type of conversation. I also think that John

may be somewhat depressed because he has been withdrawing lately. At school, all the work is centered on creative language expression, and it is clear that he would rather engage in visual graphic design or building. Thus, I have concluded that John does not have any particular disorder. However, there are a number of things that he must learn."

Developing a working theory as to why a child engages in specific "puzzling" behavior is crucial for effective intervention planning. This theory evolves as new information is gathered, and it is not necessarily 100% accurate the first time it is formulated. However, it helps you test what is called the "hypothesis." Hypotheses, as discussed earlier, are used in science to test questions based on a particular theory. For example, a long time ago, researchers developed a theory that the earth revolved around the sun. If that were true, then there would be signs in the universe that the earth is moving. A hypothesis for this example could be, "The earth can be seen moving through space by noting that the stars in the sky change nightly." The researchers could then set out to "disprove" this hypothesis. Most of the time in science, it is only possible to "disprove" a particular hypothesis rather than prove it. However, the more researchers can rule out any other competing explanations, the more they can say that the hypothesis, and thus, the theory, seem to be true.

ACTIVITY #9: THEORY BUILDING

Now it is your turn to develop a theory for your child's puzzling behavior. To complete this task, review the summary statements previously completed in Activity #7, as well as the information from Activity #8. Based on these two sets of information, incorporate what you know about the child into several sentences. Place this information on the Theory Building sheet that you partially completed in Activity #7. This form is located on page 60. In developing these sentences and

THEORY BUILDING WORKSHEET

CHILD'S NAME _____

SUMMARY STATEMENTS

Example:
Given that Denise has undergone many changes during the course of her life (e.g., changed schools three times and moved to different communities twice), when she is presented with a change in her routine, she becomes very upset and begins to tantrum and yell. In response to her yelling, her parents oftentimes will not change her schedule and stick with the original plan. It appears that Denise's tantrums serve to prevent her parents from making any more changes in her life.

Put your summary statements here:

WORKING THEORY

As you investigate more of the causes pertaining to your child's puzzling behavior, you will develop insights along the way. To build a theory as to why your child is demonstrating the behavior, you first start with your summary statement, and then modify these statements into more of a working theory. This theory is modified as new information is obtained and may be changed continuously. An example of a theory from the above summary statements is as follows:

Denise tantrums for a number of reasons, including not wanting to change her schedule or when she is having difficulty expressing herself. Since we discovered some expressive language difficulties, it is clear that she has difficulty expressing herself in a time of need.

After you have investigated other causes to your child's puzzling behavior, write a one-paragraph theory below:

Download reproducible worksheets at www.lifespanpress.com.

using the information acquired above, try to address the following questions:

1. What can you say about the child's behavior?
2. Is the behavior considered abnormal by a professional?
3. What factors contribute to the behavior?
4. What can you say about the overall reason why the child demonstrates puzzling behavior?

This may be a challenging task, but do the best you can. You can use the model presented on the Theory Building sheet and the theory generated on the previous page as guides. A good format for the theory building sentences is as follows: First, state what your child does. Second, state what you found out about your child that contributes to the puzzling behavior. Third, state why you think the child demonstrates the behavior of concern. An example is as follows:

Jill is frequently very hyperactive and gets out of control when she is tired. We have discovered that Jill is very prone to fatigue and mood difficulties. We are not sure, but we think she may have a mood disorder, such as depression. We also know that she has great difficulties controlling her impulses, but according to her pediatrician, she does not meet the diagnosis of Attention-Deficit/Hyperactivity Disorder (ADHD). In our opinion, Jill is hyperactive and becomes out of control because she is overly tired and when tired she has difficulty regulating her behavior.

A sample scenario and examples of completed forms may be found beginning on page 70.

CHILD'S PROFILE OF STRENGTHS AND WEAKNESSES

The next step to intervention planning is to develop a profile of your child's strengths and areas of need. "Areas of need" are specific aspects of the child that need growth or improvement. Examples of areas of need include improving speech articulation, improving socialization with others, or improving handwriting. These areas of need can be identified by reviewing the results of the functional behavioral assessment (FBA), results of the Causal Factors Worksheet, and by reviewing the theory that you have developed for the child. Again, these worksheets are located on pages 56 and 60. Areas of strength for the child can also be identified by reviewing these documents.

In locating areas of strength, think about the positive aspects of your child. Also think about what your child is interested in and what your child does well. Sometimes locating areas of strength can be quite challenging. However, the reader is encouraged to pay attention to the subtle aspects of the child. For example, if the child is argumentative, perhaps one area of strength is the child's verbal reasoning ability. It is challenging to argue effectively without good verbal skills. An example of a profile created for a particular child is as follows:

> Louie is a 10-year-old boy in the fourth grade who has a long history of difficulties with hyperactivity, impulsivity, and inattentiveness. He clearly meets the criteria for Attention-Deficit/Hyperactivity Disorder (ADHD). Areas of strength and weakness were identified by his mother to include the following: 1) Areas of strength include building, imitating cartoon characters, learning different languages, and singing; 2) Areas of weakness include having difficulties with thinking before acting, being aggressive toward his younger brother, and not listening in class.

By identifying a child's strengths and weaknesses, you are in fact developing a "profile" for your child. Areas of strength, as well as areas of need, are carefully articulated. This type of profile is similar to the neurodevelopmental profiles articulated by Dr. Levine.

ACTIVITY #10: PROFILE DEVELOPMENT

To complete a profile of your child, first locate the Intervention Planning Worksheet on page 65. The first step is to review the information obtained from the activities on the clarification of concerns (Activity #1), activities on functional behavioral assessment (Activities #1-7), activities on causal factors (Activity #8), and activities on theory building (Activity #9). Review this information, and complete the following steps:

1. List areas of weakness for which you plan to design an intervention. List these under the "Areas of Need/Growth" section. Try to be short and specific when you list these concerns. The rule of thumb is to also list these in positive terms. The goal is to improve upon something rather than decrease something. For example, if a child is hitting, it is best to write "increase verbal expression when angry" rather than "not hitting." It is much easier to teach a new behavior rather than take an old one away.

2. List areas of strength for which you also plan to design an intervention. List these under the "Areas of Interest/Strength" section. Again, try to be as specific as you can. The results of "A" and "B" form the completed profile for your child.

INTERVENTION PLANNING

Once you have completed the profile for your child, look over it, and note if you have any particular insights. Jot these down under the "Comments" section on the Intervention Planning Worksheet. For each of the areas of need and strength, it is best to plan a specific intervention. Thus, interventions will take place in both the areas of strength as well as the areas of need. This creates a well-rounded intervention strategy. To create specific interventions, you will need to review again the information from the previous exercises, and see what ideas come to you. A sample scenario and examples of completed forms may be found beginning on page 70.

You may be asking yourself, "How do I design an intervention?" There are many ways that interventions can be designed, and the answer to this question is actually dependent on the type of problem presented. Sometimes the interventions may be purely behavioral in focus, whereby you will have to modify some aspect of your child's puzzling behavior. At other times, the intervention may require the use of medication or some type of therapy.

One way of developing interventions is to form a team of care providers who will discuss the needs of your child with you. In the schools, teams consisting of teachers, administrators, and specialists frequently develop intervention strategies for children. If your child has a difficulty related to school, it may be helpful to set up a meeting to discuss your child with these individuals. If the difficulty is not related to school, it may still be possible to get a team meeting together, but this is not always so easy since the involved professionals may be located in different parts of your community, making it difficult for everyone to come together. What you need to do in this case is ask each care provider for their intervention strategies, and then share these with each of the other providers. This strategy will greatly increase the likelihood that all the care providers are working

INTERVENTION PLANNING WORKSHEET

CHILD'S NAME _____

CHILD'S PROFILE	INTERVENTION	PERSON(S) RESPONSIBLE
Areas of Interest/Strength		
1.		
2.		
3.		
4.		
5.		
Areas of Need/Growth		
1.		
2.		
3.		
4.		
5.		

ADDITIONAL NOTES/COMMENTS:

Download reproducible worksheets at www.lifespanpress.com.

together toward a common goal. This coordination of care is absolutely essential.

As a parent, you have to keep in mind that you are the main caregiver of your child. You cannot completely count on the professionals in your child's life to coordinate their activities with other professionals. It is best to develop intervention strategies with these professionals and then share the entire plan with all who are involved. This does not have to be a complicated process since much of the plan can be streamlined. However, the plan should be complete enough for others to get a general idea of what you are doing.

Oftentimes, puzzling behavior can be addressed through the use of behavioral interventions. In this approach, all behavior is assumed to be supported by the current environment. Further, all behavior is assumed to be amenable to change. The typical behavioral approach is to first clarify concerns and complete a functional behavioral assessment (FBA). You have done these steps already in previous activities. The next step is to intervene in the "antecedent," "behavior," or "consequences" section. For example, you may be able to prevent hitting by removing the trigger of the hitting (antecedent) in the current environment. You may also be able to modify the behavior by teaching a more desirable behavior that is incompatible with the behavior of concern. For example, for a child who yells and screams, rather than telling the child not to yell and scream, it is more effective to teach him to express himself with words in a soft tone; it is hard to talk softly and scream at the same time. Thus, the intervention for screaming is to teach children to express themselves in a softer manner but a manner that is firm and assertive. This sounds simplistic, but it works.

General and specific interventions can be found in a number of resources. I have listed resources in the back of this guide for your use. It is a good idea to glance through that list and read a few of the recommended books and/or visit the websites. When you are deciding what to do, you can combine the information gathered from these resources with the information gathered from your own and others' assessments.

Parents need to be aware of the difference between an Individualized Education Plan (IEP) and the Intervention Planning Worksheet used in this book. The IEP is a document required for children in the special education system. Every student with a disability who has qualified for special education services will have an IEP. The Intervention Planning form used in this book is not a substitute for the IEP; these are two separate documents. In my opinion, children with puzzling behavior may need both sets of documents. Such children may be found to have a disability for which educational services are needed. Thus, an IEP would then be required. However, many times children with puzzling behavior are not found to have any type of disability. Thus, these children will not be eligible for special education services. An IEP in these cases is not required. However, for both sets of children, a profile-based approach to intervention should take place. Interventions in both the areas of need and the areas of strength are imperative.

ACTIVITY #11: INTERVENTION PLANNING

When you get to this point in the process, you are now ready to design interventions for your child. You may have intervened all along in a particular area, and that is okay. You may have already instituted some type of behavior management program. You may have already begun some type of social skills instruction. In this activity, you will formalize what you may already be doing.

The first step in intervention planning is to review the information obtained in previous exercises. It is especially important to review the target areas for intervention that have already been listed on the Intervention Planning Worksheet from Activity #10. This form is located on page 65. For each area, you are to design an intervention, and briefly describe it under the "Intervention" column. The intervention section is not numbered because sometimes one intervention can address multiple areas of need or strength. A sample scenario and examples of completed forms may be found beginning on page 70.

When intervention strategies are designed, also note who is responsible for carrying out a particular strategy. This person could be the parent, teacher, or some type of professional. When this document is completed, a copy of the plan may be given to the professionals involved in the child's life.

Step #5: Plan Implementation and Evaluation

Once you have completed the plan for your child, you are now ready for the implementation. Again, in reality, you have been intervening all along with your child. There typically is not a specific date when all plans are implemented. Usually with children demonstrating puzzling behavior, plan implementation begins immediately. However, in this section, parents are encouraged to be even more systematic in their plan implementation than they have probably been thus far in the child's life. It is important when you have a child with puzzling behavior that strategies be implemented with care and that some type of evaluation method be developed. Consistency in implementation is very important. Many times parents and teachers implement strategies haphazardly and then conclude that a given strategy did not work. Many times interventions cause subtle changes that may not be perceived by the caregivers close to the child. Progress is not always easily recognized. One behavior may change, and then the parent or teacher begins complaining about another problem behavior rather than celebrating the success with the first problem behavior. This is why some type of monitoring system needs to be established to gauge progress. For example, suppose you have a child who seems to be very "needy." This child is constantly coming up to you and asking for this or that. In this case, it is a good idea to note the number of times that the child asked questions in a given time period. After you have

WEEKLY FEEDBACK LOG

CHILD'S NAME _____

The completion of this form will provide valuable feedback for the child, parent, and teacher. Parents and teachers are to mark "+," "/," or "-," based on what they have observed for the target of change during that time period. Parents rate the time periods in which they see their child. Teachers rate the time periods during the school day. The Early Morning and Late Afternoon cells are split so that parents can rate the child's behavior prior to and after school. Please share the ratings with others in order to adjust your intervention based on the progress noted. If daily ratings do not need to be broken down into specific time periods, the raters can just put an overall rating for the day in the total section.

WEEK OF _____

PEOPLE COMPLETING LOG _____

TARGET(S) _____

_____

+ = Met   / = Partially met   - = Did Not Meet

TIME FRAME	SUN	MON	TUES	WED	THURS	FRI	SAT
Early Morning							
Late Morning							
Early Afternoon							
Late Afternoon							
Evening							
TOTAL/OVERALL							

COMMENTS:

Download reproducible worksheets at www.lifespanpress.com.

implemented your intervention, again count the number of times the child asks questions, and see if you notice a difference. This will help you measure progress. Located on the previous page is a Feedback Log. This worksheet may be used to gather data as you implement your interventions.

SAMPLE SCENARIO

In the Introduction, you were presented with a 10-year-old boy, John, who demonstrated minimal eye contact and social difficulties. The mother and teacher were concerned that the child may have Asperger's Disorder. In the section on theory building, I noted a conclusion that this boy did not have Asperger's Disorder. Instead, the social difficulties of the child were primarily demonstrated around adults; with his friends, his social skills were age appropriate. Based on this scenario, I have completed worksheets as an example. Please review these completed worksheets carefully. By reviewing them, you will better understand how to complete these worksheets for your own child.

PROBLEM WORKSHEET

CHILD'S NAME _John Kingston_

In the "Behavior of Concern" column, list specific behaviors of concern. For example, "hits sister." Under the column "Specifics," note when this behavior occurs, where this behavior occurs, and how oftern this behavior occurs. Put a star by the behavior that you are most concerned about. Under "Comments or Insights," list what additional comments or insights you may have had.

BEHAVIOR OF CONCERN (e.g., hitting)	SPECIFICS (e.g., when, where, how often does the behavior occur)
1. Social difficulties	John often appears disinterested and aloof. He does not give eye contact and speaks softly. When others are chatting, he withdraws because he does not like this conversation.
2. Depression	He has been withdrawing a lot lately.
3. Poor school performance	His grades have been declining. He loves to build with Legos, and he also loves to draw. However, at school, it is all language arts oriented.
4. Argumentative at home	When asked to do anything around the house, John geets upset. We have to argue with him constantly.
5. Gets really focused on what he likes to do	John loves to build and draw. He can draw spaceships and boats for hours. However, when he is involved in these tasks, he will not switch and do other things that he does not like to do.

COMMENTS OR INSIGHTS:
He has many friendships with his peers. He seems to demonstrate social difficulties mainly around adults.

ABCs WORKSHEET

CHILD'S NAME _John Kingston_

Step 1: List behavior of concern in three words or less in "B." Step 2: List factors in "Setting Event" that contribute long term to the behavior of concern (e.g., school failure, family arguing, etc.). Step 3: List in "A" events that come immediately before the behavior of concern (e.g., directions given). Step 4: List in "C" what happens immediately after the behavior. Once these steps are completed, look for patterns and potential points for intervention and note under "Comments or Insights."

SETTING EVENT	ANTECEDENT "A"	BEHAVIOR "B"	CONSEQUENCES "C"
John is genuinely shy around adults. He has never been pushed to talk directly.	Is confronted with social situation where he is required to directly talk with others.	1. Social Difficulties —poor eye contact —minimal conversation	He is left alone and not required to participate.
John loves to do "hands-on" activities that are not traditionally school related.	Is asked to go to school, participate and interact with others directly.	2. Depression —low self-esteem —grumpy	Poor school performance. Is left alone by teachers because he has become such a challenge.
John does not like school, feels that he is not doing anything of interest, and is getting depressed.	Asked to do chores, homework, or other activity he does not want to do.	3. Argumentative —will not do chores or do things that he does not want to do	His difficult behavior causes others to leave him alone.

COMMENTS OR INSIGHTS:

His social difficulties seem to be due primarily to talking with adults. He is not like this with his friends.

Download reproducible worksheets at www.lifespanpress.com.

PROBLEM TRACKING SHEET

CHILD'S NAME _John Kingston_

Fill in this form by noting when the problem behavior of concern is typically demonstrated.

	SUNDAY	MONDAY	TUESDAY	WEDNESDAY	THURSDAY	FRIDAY	SATURDAY
Dates:							
Morning							
6:00							
6:30	OK						OK
7:00		Argues				→	
7:30							
8:00				Behavior OK at School			
8:30							
9:00							
9:30							
10:00							
10:30							
11:00							
11:30				Social with peers			
Afternoon							
12:00				However, seems			
12:30				somewhat depressed			
1:00							
1:30							
2:00							
2:30			∨		∨		
3:00							
3:30							
4:00							
4:30							
5:00							
5:30				Frequent arguing			
Evening	∨			with parents			
6:00	Argues						
6:30				Any social situation			
7:00				with adults, he is			
7:30				reluctant to interact			
8:00							
8:30	∨						∨
9:00	Sleep	Sleep	Sleep	Sleep	Sleep	Sleep	Sleep
9:30							
10:00							
10:30							
11:00							
Night							
12:00							
1:00							
2:00							
3:00							
4:00							
5:00							
5:30	∨	∨	∨	∨	∨	∨	∨

COMMENTS: _It seems that most of the difficulty centers around school dislike and interaction with adults._

Download reproducible worksheets at www.lifespanpress.com.

CHILD'S TYPICAL SCHEDULE

CHILD'S NAME _John Kingston_

Fill in this form as completely as possible with your child's typical schedule.

	SUNDAY	MONDAY	TUESDAY	WEDNESDAY	THURSDAY	FRIDAY	SATURDAY
Dates:							
Morning							
6:00	Sleep	→					→
6:30							
7:00		Wake-up	→				
7:30		Bus	→				
8:00		School	School	School	School	School	
8:30							
9:00							
9:30							
10:00							
10:30							
11:00							
11:30							
Afternoon							
12:00							
12:30							
1:00							
1:30	Free Time						Free Time
2:00							
2:30		↓	↓	↓	↓	↓	
3:00		Bus	→				
3:30		Homework	Homework	Homework	Homework	Homework	
4:00							
4:30		↓	↓	↓	↓	↓	
5:00							
5:30							
Evening							
6:00							
6:30				Free Time			
7:00							
7:30							
8:00							
8:30							
9:00	Sleep	Sleep	Sleep	Sleep	Sleep	Sleep	Sleep
9:30							
10:00							
10:30							
11:00							
Night							
12:00							
1:00							
2:00							
3:00							
4:00							
5:00							
5:30	↓	↓	↓	↓	↓	↓	↓

COMMENTS:

Download reproducible worksheets at www.lifespanpress.com.

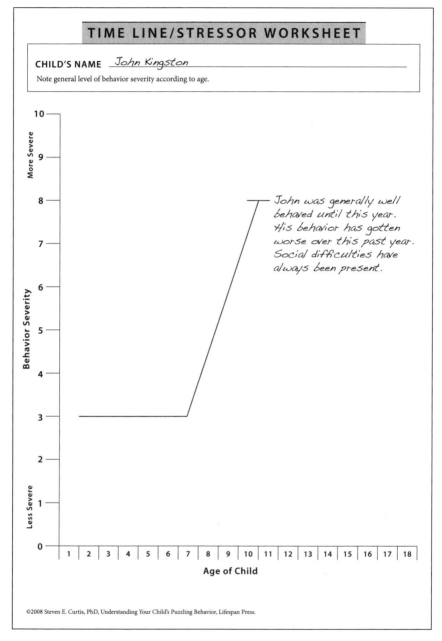

TIME LINE/STRESSOR WORKSHEET

CHILD'S NAME   *John Kingston*

Note general level of behavior severity according to age.

John was generally well behaved until this year. His behavior has gotten worse over this past year. Social difficulties have always been present.

Behavior Severity

More Severe

Less Severe

10
9
8
7
6
5
4
3
2
1
0

Age of Child

1 | 2 | 3 | 4 | 5 | 6 | 7 | 8 | 9 | 10 | 11 | 12 | 13 | 14 | 15 | 16 | 17 | 18

Download reproducible worksheets at www.lifespanpress.com.

CAUSAL FACTORS WORKSHEET

CHILD'S NAME _John Kingston_

As you investigate possible causes for your child's puzzling behavior, list the information obtained on this sheet. By completing this form, you can have a quick overview of possible contributing causes. As you complete this sheet, note any insights.

POSSIBLE FACTOR	RESULT
Medical/Developmental	He was a good baby and has been healthy his whole life. However, he has always been shy.
Hearing/Vision	No difficulties noted in this area.
Speech/Language	Attended a developmental preschool and had services for speech and language difficulties.
Sensory/Motor	Seems to enjoy being by himself or with one other person. He does not like being in large groups.
Academic/Life Skills	He has written language difficulties. He is better at math. Overall, his grades are declining.
Cognitive/Neuropsychological	He appears very bright and creative.
Emotional	He seems more down than usual. He is becoming increasingly argumentative.
Other Possible Factors	He loves building and drawing.

COMMENTS OR INSIGHTS: It seems like there were early concerns with his language that are present today.

Download reproducible worksheets at www.lifespanpress.com.

THEORY BUILDING WORKSHEET

CHILD'S NAME _John Kingston_

SUMMARY STATEMENTS

Example:
Given that Denise has undergone many changes during the course of her life (e.g., changed schools three times and moved to different communities twice), when she is presented with a change in her routine, she becomes very upset and begins to tantrum and yell. In response to her yelling, her parents oftentimes will not change her schedule and stick with the original plan. It appears that Denise's tantrums serve to prevent her parents from making any more changes in her life.

Put your summary statements here:

John is generally shy around adults and has always had difficulties with expressing himself. He prefers to be alone, or with another peer his own age, and building and drawing. He is getting depressed because he is being forced to interact with adults and complete schoolwork that he does not want to do.

WORKING THEORY

As you investigate more of the causes pertaining to your child's puzzling behavior, you will develop insights along the way. To build a theory as to why your child is demonstrating the behavior, you first start with your summary statement, and then modify these statements into more of a working theory. This theory is modified as new information is obtained and may be changed continuously. An example of a theory from the above summary statements is as follows:

Denise tantrums for a number of reasons, including not wanting to change her schedule or when she is having difficulty expressing herself. Since we discovered some expressive language difficulties, it is clear that she has difficulty expressing herself in a time of need.

After you have investigated other causes to your child's puzzling behavior, write a one-paragraph theory below:

Overall, John's social difficulties are present because he does not know what to say to adults. He is getting depressed because he does not like the work required of him at school.

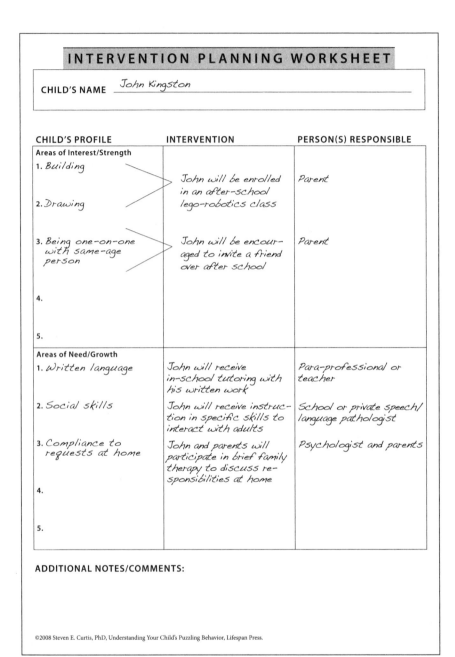

INTERVENTION PLANNING WORKSHEET

CHILD'S NAME _John Kingston_

CHILD'S PROFILE	INTERVENTION	PERSON(S) RESPONSIBLE
Areas of Interest/Strength		
1. Building	John will be enrolled in an after-school lego-robotics class	Parent
2. Drawing		
3. Being one-on-one with same-age person	John will be encouraged to invite a friend over after school	Parent
4.		
5.		
Areas of Need/Growth		
1. Written language	John will receive in-school tutoring with his written work	Para-professional or teacher
2. Social skills	John will receive instruction in specific skills to interact with adults	School or private speech/language pathologist
3. Compliance to requests at home	John and parents will participate in brief family therapy to discuss responsibilities at home	Psychologist and parents
4.		
5.		

ADDITIONAL NOTES/COMMENTS:

Download reproducible worksheets at www.lifespanpress.com.

CHAPTER FOUR

When and Where to Seek Professional Help

At What Point Should One Enlist the Help of a Professional?

You have tried everything and still you have concerns about your child's puzzling behavior. You have attempted to figure it out yourself, and you still do not quite understand what is happening. All along you have talked with friends, neighbors, and relatives. You have read books and searched the Internet. The answers to your concerns just have not revealed themselves to you. You are now asking yourself, "Should I talk to a professional? Should I take my son to see that Becky everyone talks about?"

It is time to seek professional consultation and help when you have tried everything, and you still have concerns. An appropriately trained professional may be able to assist you in finding the right answers. The professional may be able to think more objectively about your situation and let you know what to do. A professional may see something that you have failed to see. During the problem-solving process as described throughout this book, you were directed to investigate many causes for your child's puzzling behavior. Yet you can only do so much of this yourself. After much time and energy, when you have exhausted all the areas that you have personally investigated, it is time to ask a professional for help.

However, finding the right help is not easy. When more professional help is needed for your child, to whom should you turn? What type of professional should you ask for advice? As noted in the beginning of this book, when parents are in need of help, they will often turn to the provider who is recommended to them. In most cases, parents do not choose professionals in a systematic way. However, choosing the right professional at any given time is extremely important. The number and types of different professionals that you could see is staggering, and parents are often left confused regarding what to do.

There are a number of reasons for choosing the right professional. First, professionals are trained to operate in certain "competency areas." This means that they have been trained to intervene in certain situations and problem areas. When they are intervening in an area or with a particular person for which they have received no training, this is known as operating "outside the area of competence." All professionals operate outside their areas of competence from time to time, but for the most part, they should stick to what they were trained to do. If they do not have training in a particular area, they should either seek consultation from another professional or refer to someone else. Thus, it is extremely important to choose the professional who is trained to address the question you are asking. If they have no training or little experience in addressing this question, they should consult with other more appropriate professionals or refer you to the right person.

Another reason to be careful when seeking advice is that the feedback you receive is based on the vantage point of the professional. Based on the provider's profession and particular point of reference, you will receive information that is seen through a lens shaped by the provider's training, background, and experience. For instance, when you see a medical doctor, that professional will look for medical causes for the behavior. When you consult a mental health practitioner, that person will look for emotional reasons for the puzzling behavior. When you see a religious leader, that person will look at spiritual causes. When you choose a professional, be aware of their training background because then you will have some idea as to how they will view the puzzling behavior. This does not mean they will be right or wrong. It only means they will approach the puzzling behavior with that particular bias or vantage point. Ultimately, you can decide which professional is the best for you and your child, based on the type of information given to you.

Types of Care Professionals

In Table 2, I have compiled a list of the 30 most common types of professionals in the field that work with children demonstrating puzzling behavior. This list is not by any means complete. It seems that every day there is a new type of professional who is working with these children. Thus, as time passes, there will be more types of professionals involved in the field. For now, this list describes the most common professionals that are currently consulted.

As part of the list, I have included the training requirements of the profession and the website address for the national association. The web pages for national associations are often very good places to find out more about a particular profession, to get more information about a particular disorder, and to find referrals.

Prior to visiting with any type of professional, it would be a good idea to bring the information obtained from the activities in Chapter

3. If possible, give the provider this information prior to the appointment. By doing so, you will potentially save time and be more focused during your visit.

It must be noted that not all professionals and practices are accepted by other professionals in the field. The intent of these writings is not to endorse any type of professional or practice. Professionals frequently disagree over what is effective. The intent of these writings is only to describe the types of professionals that parents turn to when their child needs help. Prior to meeting with any professional, parents are strongly encouraged to research the provider's background and efficiency of the proposed treatment.

TABLE 2: TYPES OF PROFESSIONALS INVOLVED IN THE CARE OF CHILDREN WITH PUZZLING BEHAVIOR

	PROFESSIONAL TYPE & EDUCATIONAL REQUIREMENTS	VISIT FOR	ASSOCIATION WEBSITE
PROFESSIONALS TO VISIT FIRST	**General Education Teacher** **Degree:** BA, BS, MA, or MEd **Certification/License Requirement:** Teacher certification in public schools. Sometimes no certification required for private schools. **Training Post-Bachelor's:** 1 or 2 years of training in teacher education either during a bachelor's degree, as a 5th year, or as a master's degree.	Initial discussion of general concerns about your child's progress in school.	**American Education Research Association** www.aera.net **National Education Association** www.nea.org
	School Counselor **Degree:** BA, BS, MA, or MEd **Certification/License Requirement:** Counselor certification for public schools. Most times no certification required for private schools. **Training Post-Bachelor's:** 1 or 2 years of training post-bachelor's in school counseling.	Discussion of general concerns about your child's academic, behavioral, or emotional concerns.	**American School Counselor Association** www.schoolcounselor.org

	PROFESSIONAL TYPE & EDUCATIONAL REQUIREMENTS	VISIT FOR	ASSOCIATION WEBSITE
PROFESSIONALS TO VISIT FIRST	**Physician Assistant** **Degree:** Most have bachelor's degree. Earn "PA" upon completion of program. **Certification/License Requirement:** PA-C, Physician assistant certified. **Training Post-Bachelor's:** Total program is about 26 months.	Assessment/ treatment of general medical issues.	**American Academy of Physician Assistants** www.aapa.org
	Nurse Practitioner **Degree:** Master's in Nursing (MSN) **Certification/License Requirement:** APRN, Advanced practice registered nurses. **Training Post-Bachelor's:** 2 years post-bachelor's degree.	Assessment/treatment of general medical issues. Basic psychiatric and other medication management.	**American Academy of Nurse Practitioners** www.aanp.org **American Psychiatric Nurses Association** www.apna.org
	Family Practice Physician **Degree:** MD or DO **Certification/License Requirement:** Licensed physician. **Training Post-Bachelor's:** 4 years medical school. Residency in family practice medicine.	Assessment of medical issues related to puzzling behavior. Also for basic psychiatric and other medication management.	**American Academy of Family Physicians** www.aafp.org **American Academy of Osteopathy** www.academyofosteopathy.org
	Pediatrician **Degree:** MD **Certification/License Requirement:** Licensed physician. **Training Post-Bachelor's:** 4 years medical school. Residency in pediatric medicine.	Assessment of medical issues related to puzzling behavior. Also, has more experience in specific pediatric issues. Psychiatric and other medication management.	**American Academy of Pediatrics** www.aap.org
PROFESSIONALS TO VISIT NEXT	**Optometrist** **Degree:** Doctorate of Optometry (OD) **Certification/License Requirement:** Licensed optometrist with specialty in behavioral/developmental vision. **Training Post-Bachelor's:** 4 years for doctorate.	Investigation of possible vision difficulties.	**American Academy of Optometry** www.aaopt.org **American Optometric Association** www.aoa.org **College of Optometrists in Vision Development** www.covd.org **Optometric Extension Program Foundation** www.oep.org

	PROFESSIONAL TYPE & EDUCATIONAL REQUIREMENTS	VISIT FOR	ASSOCIATION WEBSITE
PROFESSIONALS TO VISIT NEXT	**Audiologist** **Degree:** master's or doctorate (AuD or PhD) **Certification/License Requirement:** CCC-A, certificate of clinical competence-audiology. **Training Post-Bachelor's:** 2 years for master's, 4 for doctorate.	Investigation of possible hearing difficulties.	**American Academy of Audiology** www.audiology.org **American Speech-Language-Hearing Association** www.asha.org
SPECIALIZED PHYSICIANS	**Developmental Pediatrician** **Degree:** MD **Certification/License Requirement:** Licensed physician. **Training Post-Bachelor's:** 4 years medical school. Pediatric residency, developmental pediatrics fellowship.	Investigation of causes/treatments of developmental issues.	**Society for Developmental and Behavioral Pediatrics** www.sdbp.org
SPECIALIZED PHYSICIANS	**Pediatric Neurologist** **Degree:** MD **Certification/License Requirement:** Licensed physician. **Training Post-Bachelor's:** 4 years medical school. Residency in pediatric neurology.	Investigation of neurological issues related to puzzling behavior.	**Child Neurology Society** www.childneurology society.org
SPECIALIZED PHYSICIANS	**Child Psychiatrist** **Degree:** MD **Certification/License Requirement:** Licensed physician. **Training Post-Bachelor's:** 4 years medical school. Residency in adult psychiatry, fellowship in child psychiatry.	Investigation of specific psychiatric issues in children.	**American Academy of Child and Adolescent Psychiatry** www.aacap.org **American Psychiatric Association** www.psych.org
MENTAL HEALTH PROVIDERS	**Child Clinical Psychologist** **Degree:** PhD **Certification/License Requirement:** Licensed psychologist. **Training Post-Bachelor's:** 4 to 5 years of graduate work plus a 1-year internship for PhD and 1-year postdoctoral training for license.	Investigation of specific psychological issues with children and for extensive psychological testing.	**American Psychological Association** www.apa.org

	PROFESSIONAL TYPE & EDUCATIONAL REQUIREMENTS	VISIT FOR	ASSOCIATION WEBSITE
MENTAL HEALTH PROVIDERS	**Neuropsychologist** **Degree:** PhD in clinical psychology or neuropsychology **Certification/License Requirement:** Licensed psychologist. **Training Post-Bachelor's:** 4 years for PhD, 1-year predoctoral internship, and 2-year postdoctoral fellowship.	Investigation of neuropsychological factors with more extensive neuropsychological testing.	**Division 40: Clinical Neuropsychology of the APA** www.div40.org **The American Academy of Clinical Neuropsychology (AACN)** www.theaacn.org
	Clinical Social Worker **Degree:** BA, MSW, or DSW **Certification/License Requirement:** LCSW (Also the ACSW, LCS, LICSW, CSW) These all indicate that the social worker is licensed. The ACSW indicates board certification. 2 years of supervised clinical work post-master's degree. **Training Post-Bachelor's:** The licensed social worker has a graduate academic degree and has completed supervised clinical work experience.	Assessment of general mental health issues—have more orientation towards family counseling.	**National Association of Social Workers** www.socialworkers.org
	Counselor **Degree:** master's degree, MA or MEd **Certification/License Requirement:** LPC (licensed professional counselor), LMHC (licensed mental health counselor), DAC (drug/alcohol counselor). **Training Post-Bachelor's:** 1 or 2 years plus several years of supervised experience for licensure. Some counselors have no training at all—make sure the counselor is licensed.	Assessment of general mental health issues.	**American Counseling Association** www.counseling.org
	Marriage & Family Therapist **Degree:** master's or doctoral degree **Certification/License Requirement:** MFCC (marriage, family, child counselor), LMFT (licensed marriage family therapist). **Training Post-Bachelor's:** At least a master's degree with post-graduate experience.	Assessment/intervention with family issues related to puzzling behavior.	**American Association for Marriage and Family Therapy** www.aamft.org
	Art Therapist **Degree:** MA or higher. **Certification/License Requirement:** ATR Board certified art therapist. **Training Post-Bachelor's:** 2 years.	Children who would benefit from intervention using artistic expression.	**American Art Therapy Association** www.arttherapy.org

	PROFESSIONAL TYPE & EDUCATIONAL REQUIREMENTS	VISIT FOR	ASSOCIATION WEBSITE
SPECIALIZED SCHOOL PROFESSIONALS	**Special Education Teacher** **Degree:** BA, MA, or MEd **Certification/License Requirement:** Certified teacher with a special education endorsement. **Training Post-Bachelor's:** Varies by state but typical training is at least 1 or 2 years in addition to general teacher certification.	Assessment of and intervention with learning and behavioral difficulties at school.	**Council for Exceptional Children** www.cec.sped.org
	School Psychologist **Degree:** MA, MEd, EdS, or PhD. Trend is to require at least the EdS degree. **Certification/License Requirement:** Certified School Psychologist. Also Nationally Certified School Psychologists (NCSP). **Training Post-Bachelor's:** 2 years post-bachelor's and 1-year internship.	Psychological and educational assessment of school related difficulties. Also can do school interventions.	**National Association of School Psychologists** www.nasponline.org
	Behavior Specialist **Degree:** No specific degree requirements. **Certification/License Requirement:** No specific license required. **Training Post-Bachelor's:** No specific requirements.	Often used in schools to help with student behavior challenges. May be a former teacher, counselor, or school psychologist.	**No specific web site**
PROFESSIONALS IN BOTH CLINICS AND SCHOOLS	**Speech/Language Pathologist (SLP)** **Degree:** MA, MS, or PhD **Certification/License Requirement:** All states require license. CCC-SLP notes the obtainment of the certificate of clinical competence. **Training Post-Bachelor's:** Master's plus year of supervised clinical experience.	Evaluation of speech/language disorders related to learning and behavior.	**American Speech-Language-Hearing Association** www.asha.org
	Occupational Therapist (OT) **Degree:** BA is entry level. In the future a master's will be required. Master of Science in Occupational Therapy (MSOT), Master of Occupational Therapy (MOT). **Certification/License Requirement:** Licensed occupational therapist (OTR/L). **Training Post-Bachelor's:** Master's degree.	Evaluation of and intervention with motor, sensory, life-skills challenges.	**American Occupational Therapy Association** www.aota.org

	PROFESSIONAL TYPE & EDUCATIONAL REQUIREMENTS	VISIT FOR	ASSOCIATION WEBSITE
PROF. IN CLINICS AND SCHOOLS	**Physical Therapist** (PT) **Degree:** Master of Physical Therapy (MPT), Doctor of Physical Therapy (DPT) **Certification/License Requirement:** Bachelor's degree for state requirements. **Training Post-Bachelor's:** At least a master's degree.	Evaluation of and intervention with gross motor difficulties.	**American Physical Therapy Association** www.apta.org
ADDITIONAL EDUCATIONAL PROFESSIONALS	**Independent Educational Consultants** **Degree:** No specific degree required, but most educational consultants have some type of degree in education, psychology, or related field. **Certification/License Requirement:** No specific license required. Certified by national association. **Training Post-Bachelor's:** Membership in professional association requires master's degree or comparable training and a minimum of 3 years experience in the position.	Excellent for learning about school-choice options, career development, or specific school issues.	**Independent Educational Consultant Association** www.educational consulting.org
	Educational Therapist **Degree:** No specific degree required. **Certification/License Requirement:** No specific state license. Certified by national association. **Training Post-Bachelor's:** No specific degree required. However, for professional membership in national association, requires education or related degree plus specific experience.	Good for children with learning challenges who need more than just basic tutoring.	**Association of Educational Therapists** www.aetonline.org
ALTERNATIVE HEALTH PROFESSIONALS	**Chiropractor** **Degree:** Doctor of Chiropractic (DC) **Certification/License Requirement:** Licensed chiropractor. **Training Post-Bachelor's:** 4 years.	Spinal health and wellness.	**American Chiropractic Association** www.amerchiro.org
	Naturopath **Degree:** Doctor of Naturopathic Medicine (ND) **Certification/License Requirement:** Varies state by state. **Training Post-Bachelor's:** 4 years.	Alternative method of healing.	**American Associations of Naturopathic Physicians** www.naturopathic.org

	PROFESSIONAL TYPE & EDUCATIONAL REQUIREMENTS	VISIT FOR	ASSOCIATION WEBSITE
ALTERNATIVE HEALTH PROF.	**Nutritionist** **Degree:** MS in Nutrition **Certification/License Requirement:** Licensed nutritionist. **Training Post-Bachelor's:** 2 years.	Investigation of nutrition issues related to puzzling behavior.	**International and American Associations of Clinical Nutritionists** www.iaacn.org **American Dietetic Association** www.eatright.org
OTHER TYPES OF PROFESSIONALS	**Parent Coach** **Degree:** No degree required. **Certification/License Requirement:** Certified by training programs—no specific state license. **Training Post-Bachelor's:** Training programs generally are about 6 months.	Good for issues relating to general parenting.	**Academy for Coaching Parents International** www.academyfor coachingparents.com
	Religious Leaders **Degree:** Requirements vary by religion. Many have an MA in Ministry. Others have the DMin (Doctorate in Ministry). **Certification/License Requirement:** No specific license required—varies by religion. **Training Post-Bachelor's:** 2 years for MA and 3 to 5 for DMin.	For counseling from a particular religious point of view and/or to investigate spiritual underpinnings of puzzling behavior.	**Association of Theological Schools** www.ats.edu

Professionals to See First

If your child is demonstrating puzzling behavior, one of the first steps is to talk with those professionals who are naturally a part of your child's life. These professionals may include general education teachers, school counselors, and your healthcare providers. These professionals see all types of children with "normal" and "puzzling" behavior. Often they can quickly tell if something seems unusual.

GENERAL EDUCATION TEACHERS

Unless the parents have home-schooled their child without assistance from any school, almost all children have at least one general education teacher in their lives. General education teachers are trained to work within the mainstream classrooms. They work in both public and private settings and deliver the majority of education throughout the world. Their function is to teach a group of children the curriculum chosen by either the teacher or the school. Teachers have a tremendous responsibility because they have to meet the needs of a large number of students and often have little outside support to do so.

The training of general education teachers varies from state to state and around the world. One might expect teacher training to be standardized across regions, just as medical school training is across many parts of the world. However, teacher training is not standardized, and each state in the US has different requirements. Individual school requirements also vary. The public sector is traditionally very strict in what it requires of teachers; usually, teachers need actual state certification. Sometimes public school systems hire teachers without any formal teacher training, but this is typically on an emergency basis because no fully certified teacher is available. Some private schools do not require teachers to be certified. In fact, some hire individuals who have little prior training but have experience working with children as well as a desire to learn more. These teachers then train as they go along.

When you do contact a general education teacher about your child, think about the training background and experience of the teacher. Is this teacher certified? If so, where did the training occur? How much experience does this teacher have? The answers to these questions are important. Teacher certification does not necessarily make someone a good teacher. But in order to achieve teacher certification, the individual must meet several criteria. More often than not, certified teachers have been specifically trained to teach children and have demonstrated their newly acquired competencies under supervision. The certified teacher most likely was taught professional ethics and learned some of the reasons behind puzzling behavior.

The type of teacher training is also important. Some programs are "fly-by-night operations," teaching large numbers of potential teachers on the weekends and providing minimal supervision when these individuals actually begin working with children. Other teacher training programs are very rigorous, and future teachers are closely supervised throughout the school day.

Experience also plays a role in the knowledge base of a teacher. An individual who has been teaching for many years clearly will have a much larger knowledge base than a teacher who has been teaching only a year. This does not mean that the new teacher has nothing to say. It only means that the more experienced teacher will have a longer history with children in the educational system from which to draw when talking about your child.

It is good to contact the teacher first when considering professional help, because he or she is able to see your child in comparison to the other children at school. This is one perspective that other specialists do not have. Few professionals listed in Table 2 have any experience working with children in a school setting or working with children in the mainstream.

SCHOOL COUNSELORS

School counselors are present in many schools and have varied roles, but typically they work with the student body at large to help ensure that the students' academic, social, and emotional needs are being met. Throughout the day, examples of counselor tasks include helping children with their schedules, meeting with parents about concerns, teaching social skills in particular classrooms, dealing with conflict between students, or providing brief counseling to students in need. Their job description is vast and varied, depending on the school culture and population with which they are faced.

School counselors see a large number of children on a daily basis and thus are good professionals with whom to consult about your child. In contrast to the specialists listed below, but similar to a teacher's experience, school counselors see not only children with puzzling behavior, but also children with more "normal" behavior. Thus, they are able to compare your child's behavior with a large number of other children's. Most specialists see only children with puzzling behavior and as a result, they can get a bit skewed in the way they view children. For example, suppose you think your child is odd socially. You can ask your school counselor about your child's social skills, and the school counselor can then compare the behavior in question with that of other children. One challenge with school counselors is that they may have limited time to address complex issues, given that they see so many children.

All states require school counselors to hold a school counseling certification and to have completed at least some graduate course work. Most require the completion of a master's degree. Some states require public school counselors to have both counseling and teaching certificates and to have had some teaching experience before receiving certification.

MEDICAL PHYSICIANS (FAMILY PRACTICE AND PEDIATRICIANS)

One of the first steps in the understanding of puzzling behavior is to investigate any medical factors that could be contributing to the behavior. If your child has complex issues, it is recommended that you start with a pediatrician or family practice physician. You can start with other medical professionals, such as nurse practitioners or physician assistants, but in many cases, children with complex behaviors need more expertise than these two professionals can provide.

The majority of medical professionals have a MD (Doctor of Medicine). This reflects that the physician has completed the basic medical school requirements. However, some physicians have a Doctor of Osteopathy or DO, indicating they have graduated from a school of osteopathy. These physicians are called "osteopaths." The training of MDs and DOs is fairly similar, but the training in osteopathy includes more attention to the use of spinal manipulation as a tool for healing. Both types of physicians complete 4 years of medical school, an internship, and a residency. Many residencies include the internship in the training. Both types of physicians are able to provide a full range of basic medical care. In addition, most physicians are now required to be board certified in their specialty area, and all physicians are required to engage in ongoing continual medical education.

Family Physicians. When you have a child with puzzling behavior and you have concerns, typically the professional to see first is your family physician or pediatrician. Family physicians are medical doctors who have training in family practice medicine. This includes broad medical training across a variety of different age groups. The majority of family physicians have completed a residency in family practice medicine, but there are still those physicians in the field who are "general practitioners." These are physicians who completed basic medical training, as well as a medical internship. However, they did not complete their residency training. These types of physicians are becoming increasingly rare since the majority of new physicians complete the residency requirement. When working with children with puzzling behavior, you want a family physician who has completed the basic residency requirements and who is board certified.

Pediatricians. An alternative to the family physician is the pediatrician. Pediatricians are medical doctors who have specialized medical training in working with children and adolescents. They may be less focused on working with the entire family but will have a much more specialized knowledge base for how to work with a particular child. Pediatricians have completed the 4 years of medical school, the 1-year internship, and the 2 years of residency. The residency may actually be 3 years, which includes the 1-year internship. Their training has focused on evaluating and treating medical issues in children. Typically, if the family practice physician has questions about a particular child, she or he will first consult with the pediatrician before referring out to other specialists.

OTHER MEDICAL PROVIDERS

Physician Assistants. Physician assistants (PAs) are healthcare professionals who practice medicine with physician supervision. PAs perform a variety of duties, including conducting physical exams, diagnosing and treating medical difficulties, and in most states, writing prescriptions. A physician assistant-certified (PA-C) means that the professional met the educational requirements and passed a test by the National Commission of Certification of Physician Assistants (NCCPA). The average PA training program curriculum lasts approximately 26 months.

Nurse Practitioners. A nurse practitioner (NP) is a registered nurse with training in the diagnoses and treatment of common illnesses. Nurse practitioners can function independently to provide many of the same services as physicians, including the prescription of medication in most states. Nurse practitioners typically have a master's degree that includes intensive clinical training under the supervision of a physician or an experienced nurse practitioner. There are an increasing number of nurse practitioners in private practice who are providing both general and specialized medical care. Further, some but not all nurse practitioners have specialized in the area of mental health. These NPs can provide both psychotherapy and medication management if needed.

Professionals to See Next

The family practice physicians, pediatricians, and other medical providers will have at their disposal a number of referral sources. These providers are accustomed to being the first to see the child with puzzling behavior. They have also spent quite a bit of time thinking about where to refer if they find they need either more information or help in working with a particular problem behavior.

When trying to figure out the puzzling behavior of these children, usually one professional will make a referral to another professional. Sometimes a child will be referred for basic counseling. At other times, the child will be referred for more specialized medical testing. The next type of individual to be seen really depends on the particular issue that is presented. Below is a list of possibilities. Of course, you will not be seeing all of these professionals. The type chosen will depend on the reason for the visit. In Table 2 is a brief description of the reasons why you would see a particular professional. The information in the table, as well as the information presented below, will help you decide whom to see next.

OPTOMETRISTS

At times children may experience behavioral or learning problems because of vision difficulties. Even though your child may have had a vision screening with a school nurse or with your physician, it is imperative that you take your child to an optometrist for a full vision and eye health checkup if puzzling behavior is a concern. Optometrists frequently do much more extensive vision examinations than those given by physicians or nurses. Your child may have a subtle vision difficulty that was not detected earlier. Examining vision is much more than just looking at whether the child can see 20/20. Evaluating the entire system is the key. It is best to take your child to an optometrist who has a specialization in developmental (behavioral) optometry (see below).

Optometrists have a doctorate in optometry and have specialized in studying and conducting intervention with the visual system. Some optometrists have specialized in helping individuals who have learning difficulties because of vision skills deficits. These are called "developmental optometrists," and they help by prescribing different types of lenses and conducting visual training so that such difficulties can be corrected. Developmental optometrists are also called behavioral optometrists. In general, developmental optometrists seem to look more at the whole child instead of just the eyes. Developmental optometrists will often do some developmental testing, such as visual skill testing relevant to reading, writing, and math.[10]

There seem to be fewer optometrists who are specializing in developmental optometry. Parents are encouraged to do a search on the Internet for qualified practitioners, using the web addresses listed in Table 2 under "optometrists."

AUDIOLOGISTS

Audiologists examine and work with people who have hearing and balance difficulties. Audiologists use a variety of testing devices to assess an individual's ability to hear sounds, distinguish between sounds, and maintain a sense of balance. They are very experienced in determining whether hearing difficulties are one of the causal factors behind puzzling behavior. The origin of hearing difficulties can be found in the inner, middle, or outer ear. Typically, someone who has trouble hearing sounds will have some type of sensorineural nerve damage in the inner ear (cochlea). In other situations, the individual will have trouble in the middle ear related to ear infections, possible disease processes, or congenital malformation. In still other circumstances, an individual may have some type of ear canal malfunction or obstruction. Any defect in or damage to the outer, middle, or inner ear can cause hearing challenges.

Impairments may also be due to some type of difficulty along the auditory nerve and/or in the auditory cortex. In these cases, individuals may be able to hear sounds but may have trouble discriminating between sounds and interpreting the sounds they perceive. An individual with significant difficulties in this area could be diagnosed

---

[10] As a side note, there are also pediatric ophthalmologists. Pediatric ophthalmologists are medical doctors who specialize in the visual system. They are experts in the assessment of eyes but seem to stop at the level of the optic nerve. This means they tend to focus on specific physical pathologies as opposed to making a holistic evaluation of the visual system and the child.

with a "Central Auditory Processing Disorder" or CAPD. Children with CAPD often do not recognize subtle differences between sounds in words, even though the sounds themselves are heard clearly. These kinds of challenges are more likely to occur when a person with CAPD is in a noisy environment or when the child is exposed to a large amount of complex language. Audiologists can help to diagnose and intervene with this problem.

Audiologists are required to have at least a master's degree in audiology. An increasing number of audiologists hold a doctorate (e.g., in audiology or philosophy [i.e., a PhD]). Further, audiologists often acquire the Certificate of Clinical Competence in Audiology (CCP-A) offered by the American Speech-Language-Hearing Association. Audiologists may also be certified through the American Board of Audiology.

As with optometrists, audiologists perform much more extensive evaluations than those given by typical physicians or school nurses. It is my experience that children can pass the hearing screenings at school and still have hearing impairments, as their particular problem may be very subtle and difficult to detect. When you have a child who has difficulty paying attention or who seems to have trouble following directions, a comprehensive evaluation by a qualified audiologist experienced with children is certainly recommended.

SPECIALIZED PHYSICIANS

If your child demonstrates behavioral or developmental challenges that are beyond the expertise of the family practice physician or pediatrician, you may be asked to take your child to one of the specialized physicians below. These physicians are often located in university medical centers, but they are also found in other outpatient clinics and private practice settings.

Developmental Pediatricians. Developmental pediatricians are medical doctors who have completed medical school, a residency in pediatrics, and an additional fellowship in developmental pediatrics. These physicians are specialists in the diagnosis and management of children with abnormal conditions that are associated with development. For example, developmental pediatricians are experts in the diagnosis of Autistic Disorder. Not only can they diagnose Autistic Disorder, they can also investigate genetic and other medical factors that could be related to the observed developmental delays.

Developmental pediatricians are wonderful resources, especially for parents of children who fall in the range between the early stages of development and adolescence. Thus, when the family physician or pediatrician has concerns about the development of the child, they will often refer to a developmental pediatrician for further evaluation.

Pediatric Neurologists. A pediatric neurologist is a physician who specializes in evaluation and treatment of: (1) nerves of the head; (2) muscle strength and movement; (3) balance, ambulation, and reflexes; and (4) sensation, memory, speech, language, and other cognitive abilities. These examinations might include such diagnostic tests as (1) CAT scans (computed axial tomography), (2) MRI/MRA (magnetic resonance imaging/magnetic resonance angiography), (3) EEG (electroencephalography), and (4) EMG (electromyography). The typical training of a pediatric neurologist is 4 years of medical school, a 1-year internship, 2 to 3 additional years of pediatric medical training (or 3 years of residency, which includes the internship), and then a 3-year residency program in pediatric neurology.

Pediatric neurologists are commonly consulted when assessing preschool and school-age children who are demonstrating unusual behavior that is thought to be sensory or neurological in nature. Their approach to the evaluation of a child with puzzling behavior will be to evaluate the functioning of the nervous system. With their expertise, these professionals can determine the presence of such conditions as seizure disorders, nerve damage, or other neurological disorders.

Child Psychiatrists. Child psychiatrists are medical doctors who have specialized in the diagnosis and treatment of children with emotional and behavioral difficulties. Child psychiatrists have completed medical school, a 1-year medical internship, a 3-year residency in adult psychiatry, and a 2-year fellowship in child psychiatry. Thus, child psychiatrists not only work with children, they also can work with adults. Child psychiatrists are different from child clinical psychologists (see below) because the child psychiatrist has an MD (Doctor of Medicine), and the child clinical psychologist has a PhD (Doctor of Philosophy). Child psychiatrists can prescribe medication and order a variety of medical procedures. Child psychiatrists are needed when children present with unusually complex behaviors and/or when the medical treatment of a psychiatric condition is outside the comfort zone of the general medical provider.

Differences Between Specialized Medical Providers

The differences between developmental pediatricians, pediatric neurologists, and child psychiatrists can be large and small at the same time. Each of these specialized physicians has a separate, as well as a shared, set of competencies. All three are able to evaluate your child's puzzling behavior and prescribe medication. However, each one is also very different. For example, developmental pediatricians are experts in normal and abnormal pediatric development. They have much experience working with both normal children, as well as those who present with puzzling behavior. They are also proficient with the determination of such developmental difficulties as Autistic Disorder or the reasons for feeding difficulties. Pediatric neurologists also know about child development, but they are more focused on the neurological aspects of a child. Their expertise is in assessing both obvious as well as more subtle neurological difficulties. Child psychiatrists also share commonalities with the developmental pediatrician and pediatric neurologist. However, the child psychiatrist is an expert in examining the emotional condition of the child and intervening with medication or talk therapy techniques.

Given this information, to whom should you turn? If you have concerns about your child's general level of development, it is recommended to first consult a developmental pediatrician. The pediatrician can then refer to another provider if the concern is better addressed by another professional's area of expertise. If you have concerns about the neurological condition of your child, then it would be advisable to consult a pediatric neurologist. Finally, if you feel your child's emotional condition might benefit from medication, then it would be appropriate to consult a child psychiatrist. However, prior to consulting any of these specialized medical professionals, it would be prudent to discuss these concerns with your family practice physician or pediatrician first. In addition, whom you see could depend upon the availability of the clinician. Each of these specialists is often quite busy.

MENTAL HEALTH PRACTITIONERS

When your child's puzzling behavior is not seen as due to medical, vision, or hearing difficulties, you may be referred to a provider who specializes in the field of mental health. Mental health clinicians are experts in working with people whose psychological challenges impact their daily lives in some manner. In the field of mental health, there are a number of different types of providers who can help, including psychiatrists, psychologists, social workers, some nurse practitioners, and specialized counselors. Psychiatrists and nurse practitioners were described above; the remaining disciplines will be discussed below. Again, which provider you consult depends on the question you are trying to answer.

Psychologists. Psychologists are experts in the study of human behavior. The focus of their training and experience has been on understanding what people do. There are a variety of psychologists who are employed in a wide range of settings. Different types of psychologists include the following: (1) research psychologists, (2) school psychologists, (3) counseling psychologists, (4) industrial/organizational psychologists, and (5) clinical psychologists. Research psychologists are behind much of the information that we have learned about children with puzzling behavior. These psychologists are typically employed in university settings. Most research psychologists primarily engage in research activities and do not see patients on a regular basis. School psychologists study the learning and behavior of children in the school environment, and are typically employed in school settings. Counseling psychologists are experts in a wide range of life adjustment difficulties and are typically employed in university counseling centers, mental health centers, and private practice. Industrial/organizational psychologists are experts in working with adults in the work force. These psychologists are often employed in large companies, especially in human resource departments.

Clinical psychologists are experts in the diagnosis and treatment of individuals with more significant mental health issues. These psychologists are often employed in hospitals, mental health centers, and private practice. Child clinical psychologists have additional expertise in working with children demonstrating puzzling behavior. Clinical neuropsychologists have specialized training in the assessment and treatment of a variety of conditions related to the brain-behavior relationship.

In order to be called a "psychologist," the individual must have a doctoral degree in either philosophy or psychology (e.g., PhD or PsyD).[11] The one exception is for psychologists working in the school system as school psychologists, who are only required to have a master's degree or educational specialist degree (EdS) (see training requirements under "specialized school professional" in Table 2). A doctoral degree generally requires 5 to 7 years of graduate study. The PhD culminates in a dissertation, which is based on original research. The PsyD is based on practical work experiences and examinations

---

[11] Even though the PhD is called a "Doctor of Philosophy", this does not mean that the psychologist with a PhD is a philosopher. Psychologists with either the PhD or the PsyD have similar and specific training in psychology.

rather than a dissertation. In clinical or counseling psychology, the requirements for the doctoral degree include at least a 1-year internship. The American Psychological Association (APA) is the accrediting organization for doctoral training programs in clinical, counseling, and school psychology. The National Association of School Psychologists (NASP) is the accreditation body for programs that focus only on school psychology.

Psychiatrists, as described above, evaluate and treat a variety of conditions with medication and psychotherapy. Psychologists, in turn, evaluate and treat many of the same conditions that psychiatrists treat, but they primarily use psychotherapy. Psychologists are specially trained to conduct psychological testing, which other mental health professionals cannot do. Historically, psychologists have not had medication prescription privileges. However, this is changing. States are beginning to grant prescription authority to specially trained psychologists. At the present time, New Mexico and Louisiana are the only states granting these privileges, but other states are considering doing so as well.

Social Workers. Social workers work in a variety of government and private agencies, as well as in private practice. They can work with individuals or groups, or they can work at a systems level with families, agencies, or communities. Social workers do a variety of tasks, one of which is counseling. Those who provide counseling on a regular basis have specialized in the field of mental health.

Only those who have earned social work degrees at the bachelor's, master's, or doctoral levels and have completed a minimum number of hours in supervised fieldwork are considered "professional social workers." A master's degree in social work (MSW) is typically required for mental health clinical work. Some social workers have doctoral degrees, and many of these professionals work in university teaching settings. Most states require at least 2 years of supervised clinical experience for licensure. In addition, the National Association of Social Workers (NASW) credentials social workers on a national level.

Social workers with an MSW may qualify for the Academy of Certified Social Workers (ACSW), the Qualified Clinical Social Worker (QCSW), or the Diplomate in Clinical Social Work (DCSW) credential, based on their professional experience.

Counselors. Psychologists, psychiatrists, and the other mental health professionals described in this guide have "counseling" as one of the services they provide. However, they may or may not call themselves a "counselor." The term "counselor" can describe a number of professionals, such as school counselors (described above), substance abuse counselors, career counselors, and mental health counselors. Counselors work in a variety of settings, including schools, mental health centers, university counseling clinics, and private practice.

Most trained counselors have at least a master's degree in a field such as counseling, psychology, or substance abuse treatment and generally must complete 2 years of supervised practice before obtaining a license for independent practice. The title of the license varies by state. For example, in the State of Washington, licensed counselors are called "Licensed Mental Health Counselors" (LMHC). In some states, counselors can enter into private practice and call themselves "counselor" with no credential at all. The consumer needs to be aware of this fact and be cautious about entering into therapeutic relationships with a counselor who has had no systematic training or supervision in the field.

Marriage and Family Therapists. Marriage and family therapists are specialized counselors who focus their practice on married people and families. They also work with individuals in the context of family relationships. Typically, in order to be a marriage and family therapist, an individual must have at least a master's or doctoral degree in the field, with additional supervised post-graduate experience.

Registered Art Therapists. Art therapists are also specialized counselors who work with people using art as the medium of expression. They often work as part of a team in settings such as hospitals, schools, and private practice. In order to be considered an art therapist, the individual must have a master's degree in art therapy or a related field.

SPECIALIZED SCHOOL PROFESSIONALS

When you have a child with puzzling behavior, it is not uncommon for your child to be evaluated by a number of clinicians within the school setting. This evaluation is most typically conducted for possible special education services. When a child is evaluated for special education services, the team must include a general education teacher, special education teacher, an administrator, someone who can give appropriate tests, and someone who can interpret the test results. Professionals involved in this process, other than the administrators and teachers, often include school psychologists, speech/language pathologists, and occupational therapists. All these professionals work as a team to determine eligibility for special education services and what types of intervention the child needs. Special education teachers and school psychologists almost exclusively work in school systems. Speech/language pathologists, occupational therapists, and physical therapists are regularly employed in school systems. However, these three professionals are also found in settings outside the school system, such as private practice clinics and medical centers. Independent educational consultants and educational therapists work primarily in private practice.

Special Education Teachers. A special education teacher is a professional who has specialized in working with children with special needs. These teachers work directly with students, collaborate with general education teachers, and often manage a team of paraprofessionals who are providing services to a number of students in need. These teachers are specialists in working with such difficulties as reading delays, cognitive delays, or behavioral challenges. Special education teachers provide much of the instruction as mandated by the student's special education individualized education plan (IEP).

If your child receives special education services, then most likely the special education teacher will be providing specialized instruction.

The requirements to be a special education teacher vary by state. However, special education teachers must be certified teachers with additional training in the field of special education. All special education teachers have at least a bachelor's degree, and many hold a master's degree. The well-trained special education teacher will have graduated from a master's degree program that is accredited by the Council for Exceptional Children.

School Psychologists. School psychologists evaluate and intervene with children who demonstrate learning and behavioral challenges in the school setting. They are most widely used for their evaluation services to determine if a student qualifies for special education services. However, school psychologists are trained to do much more than just evaluate students. School psychologists are trained in counseling and classroom intervention. A school psychologist may be called in if behavioral challenges surface. If your child is referred for special education services, the school psychologist will be the leader of the evaluation team.

A school psychologist is the one type of psychologist that does not require a doctoral degree. The standard expectation is that all school psychologists will have at least the educational specialist degree (EdS) in school psychology. This degree is beyond that typically required for a master's degree but less than that typically required for a doctoral degree. Many school psychologists hold the EdS degree, some hold a master's degree in education, and others hold a doctoral degree in school psychology. The EdS is considered in between a master's and doctoral degree. School psychologists who have met the training requirements of the National Association of School Psychologists will be considered nationally certified school psychologists and thus hold the NCSP designation (Nationally Certified School Psychologist).

Behavior Specialists. A behavior specialist is the title given to the school employee who has the primary responsibility of intervening with children who demonstrate behavioral challenges. Employees hired as behavior specialists will consult with teachers, function as members of behavior intervention teams, and work individually with students of concern. The job responsibilities of this position vary by school system. Some schools may use an alternative title, such as "behavior interventionist" or "behavior support specialist."

There are no particular requirements for being a behavior specialist. This is not typically a certified position (i.e., the individual hired for this position does not need special training). However, most individuals who are employed in this position hold at least a bachelor's degree, and many hold a master's degree. Many are certified teachers, and some are counselors. Because of these variations, it is important to understand the background and training of the particular behavior specialist when working with one. A behavior specialist might be involved in your child's education if your child displays frequent puzzling behavior during the school day.

PROFESSIONALS IN BOTH CLINICS AND SCHOOLS

Speech-Language Pathologists.[12] Speech-language pathologists (SLPs) work with a broad range of disorders affecting speech, language, cognition, memory, swallowing, voice and social communication, and interaction for children and adults. Roughly half of SLPs work in school settings, with difficulties affecting a child's educational goals. The other half work in medical clinics, private practice, research, social service agencies, and university settings. Your child may work with a speech-language pathologist at school if speech or language skills have been targeted as areas of need.

Speech-language pathologists have at least a master's degree. Some have obtained a PhD. In most states, speech-language pathologists must comply with state standards for licensure, which are very similar to the standards set by the Council for Clinical Certification (CFCC) of

---

[12] Speech-language pathologists, occupational therapists, and physical therapists are found in both schools and other settings, such as private clinics and medical centers.

the American Speech Hearing Association (ASHA). Speech-language pathologists who are fully credentialed by ASHA place a "SLP-CCC" after their name, indicating a certificate of clinical competence.

Occupational Therapists. Occupational therapists (OTs) help people with physical, medical, or emotional challenges cope and/or recover their ability to conduct daily living skills and function in working environments so they can live independent lives. They can assist individuals with such activities as dressing, cooking, eating, walking, and engaging in fine motor tasks. Occupational therapists work in a variety of settings, including hospitals, outpatient clinics, and private practice. Some occupational therapists may work exclusively with children. When working in schools, occupational therapists evaluate children's abilities and then recommend interventions, which might include modifying the classroom environment or curriculum. Your child may work with an occupational therapist if the child has fine or gross motor difficulties, daily life-skill challenges, or sensory difficulties.

Most occupational therapists have a master's degree. To obtain a license, applicants must graduate from an accredited educational program and pass a national certification examination. Those who pass the exam are awarded the title "Occupational Therapist Registered" (OTR). Registered occupational therapists who are also licensed use the title "OTR/L".

Physical Therapists. Physical therapists (PTs) are healthcare professionals who evaluate and treat people with medical or health-related problems resulting from injury or disease that affect their abilities to perform the functional activities of daily living. Physical therapists assess joint motion, muscle strength and endurance, function of heart and lungs, and performance of activities required in daily living, among other responsibilities. Treatments include a broad range of techniques, such as manual therapies of deep myofascial release and joint mobilization to increase mobility, therapeutic exercise techniques to improve strength and stability, neuromuscular re-education to develop improved muscle coordination and mechanics, adaptation techniques and assistive devices if needed, training to return to activities of daily living, programs to decrease disabilities, plus cardiovascular and endurance training. Other therapies used are the modalities of ultrasound, electrical stimulation, and cold lasers to promote tissue healing. Therapy is geared toward individuals who have injuries or disease processes causing neurological deficits. Physical therapists using multiple techniques, both manual and exercise, encourage patients to use their muscles and joints to progress through programs designed to increase flexibility, strength, balance, endurance, and coordination, with the goal of ultimately restoring a higher level of function.

Physical therapists work in a variety of settings. Some are generalists and treat a variety of disabilities. Others specialize in areas such as pediatrics, orthopedics, and neurology. Physical therapists who work in the schools help provide quality educational opportunities for children in need. Your child may work with a physical therapist at school if gross motor difficulties are of concern.

All physical therapists must have a graduate degree from an accredited physical therapy program and have passed a state licensing exam. All new graduates must have a master's degree or a doctorate in physical therapy.

ADDITIONAL EDUCATIONAL PROFESSIONALS

Independent educational consultants assist parents in assessing their child's academic, emotional, and behavioral difficulties, and help find the right place for their child. Not all consultants work with children who have emotional and behavioral difficulties, so it is important to locate a consultant who specializes in "special purpose" schools and programs.

The majority of independent educational consultants around the country are members of the Independent Educational Consultant Association (IECA). It would be advisable for parents to work with those consultants who hold memberships with this organization. Although there are no state licensure requirements, IECA membership requires a master's degree or equivalent, or comparable training. A minimum of 3 years experience in the profession is required for membership with IECA. Members of IECA meet the organization's professional standards and subscribe to its Principles of Good Practice.

IECA members are required to visit a number of programs annually, keeping abreast of the quality and diversity of programs and schools across the country. Members maintain and update their knowledge of diverse programs and schools through visitations, workshops, training programs, and information exchanges with colleges, schools, programs, and other consultants.

Important to parents, IECA consultants contract with parents, not schools or programs. The consultants work for the parents and do not have interests in the programs and schools to which they refer. The consultants avoid multiple relationships that could harm or raise questions about the integrity of a consultant's relationships with families. Special purpose consultants work to learn as much as possible about the family and the child, using other professionals in the community to achieve a comprehensive profile of the child, and then match his or her needs, strengths, weaknesses, and interests in order to help the child reach his or her full potential. Although many consultants work with those students who have emotional and behavior problems, as well as those who have learning disabilities, others assist families in college prep schools or summer enrichment programs, as well as help in college or university selection.

Educational Therapists. Educational therapists provide intensive educational intervention to children and adults with learning challenges. They differ from tutors in that they attend to the individual's psychological and educational needs versus merely focusing on the educational needs alone. This is important because at times learning difficulties have both an academic and an emotional component. Thus, an educational therapist can address both. You may wish to employ an educational therapist if traditional tutoring has failed to produce longstanding results. Most work in private practice.

There are no particular legal requirements to be an "educational therapist." However, in order to be a professional member of the Association of Educational Therapists, an individual must (1) possess a master's degree (or have taken sufficient graduate level and/or upper division level courses); (2) have provided educational therapy in private practice, public or private schools, private clinics, hospitals, or public agencies; and (3) have met the direct service delivery minimum of 1,500 hours.

ALTERNATIVE HEALTHCARE PROFESSIONALS

Chiropractors. Chiropractors are alternative, primary care physicians who diagnose and treat health problems that are related to the body's musculoskeletal and nervous systems. Chiropractic medicine is based on the concept that bodily functions can be impaired by difficulties with the spinal cord and vertebrae. Chiropractors focus their attention on the spine to promote overall physical health. A fundamental aspect of their practice is manipulating or adjusting the spinal column to alleviate problems from misaligned vertebrae. Chiropractors diagnose patients' conditions based on their medical history, a physical exam, data from testing, and diagnostic imaging. Then they often incorporate a number of alternative remedies into their general patient care, including nutrition advice, acupuncture, or herbal medicine. A chiropractor may be consulted if a child's puzzling behavior could be potentially improved by the promotion of spinal and physical wellness.

Licensed chiropractors must have a doctorate degree in chiropractic (DC) degree, which involves 4 years of science and clinical training. Some of the core course work is similar to a typical MD curriculum (including topics such as genetics, microbiology, and radiology). However, the chiropractic curriculum differs from traditional health-related course work in two ways: First, due to the profession's tenets, as well as the restrictions on a DC's scope of practice, chiropractors are not trained in pharmacology, surgery, or other invasive or specialty techniques; DC programs focus entirely on noninvasive, primary care medicine. Secondly, DC programs have an increased focus on alternative therapies, such as nutrition, hygiene, acupuncture, exercise, botanical medicine, and stress management.

Naturopaths. Naturopathic physicians treat and manage a broad range of health conditions using a holistic philosophy, traditional therapies, and information obtained from advances in modern medicine. Naturopaths are often consulted about children who demonstrate attention problems or depression. Some parents do not agree with the mainstream medical treatment of these difficulties and seek a more natural remedy. Naturopaths are known to treat attention and mood difficulties in a more homeopathic manner.

Naturopaths have a doctorate in naturopathy (ND), and their training involves learning about basic medical sciences and conventional diagnostics. Training components also include the following: (1) therapeutic nutrition, (2) botanical medicine, (3) homeopathy, (4) natural childbirth, (5) classical Chinese medicine, (6) hydrotherapy, (7) naturopathic manipulative therapy, (8) pharmacology, and (9) minor surgery.

Nutritionists. Nutritionists are experts in the planning and supervision of food and nutrition programs. They can help treat illness and promote wellness by encouraging healthy eating habits and dietary modifications. Nutritionists may be involved in the care of the child with puzzling behavior because issues related to food (e.g., food allergies) may be seen as impacting learning and behavior. These professionals are mainly employed in healthcare facilities on an inpatient or outpatient basis. For licensure, most nutritionists hold a master's degree.

OTHER TYPES OF PROFESSIONALS

Parent Coaches. A parent coach is a personal coach who specializes in parent/child issues. When a parent or other caregiver needs assistance with a parenting issue, they can hire a parent coach, who can help parents and caregivers by listening, problem-solving, and offering advice. Licensure is not required to be a parent coach. However, most are certified by the Academy for Coaching Parents International. This certification takes about 6 months, depending on the individual's background and experience.

Religious Leaders. Parents of children with puzzling behavior often consult with their pastor, priest, rabbi, or other religious leader about their concerns. In fact, in many parts of the world, consulting with a religious leader is the first step a parent with a child with puzzling behavior takes. Prior to the 1900s, most people in the Western world consulted with religious leaders. But as the medical profession has gained prominence, this trend has changed. Now many of these same people are turning to medical providers first. But it is important to remember that some people still will turn to their religious leader first for help.

The training of religious leaders varies, depending on the religious institution. Some religious leaders have extensive training in counseling, while others do not. Many in the United States have a Doctor of Ministry (DMin) degree, an advanced professional degree for those in the practice of ministry. It differs from a PhD in that its focus is on competence in religious practices rather than on advanced academic research.

The Power of Team Collaboration

You will find that it will be practically impossible, and not advisable, to consult with more than a handful of the providers described above. You will reach a point in your journey where you feel that you have gained sufficient knowledge, are totally confused, or have no interest in seeking any more opinions. This is a normal response for parents of children with puzzling behavior who are searching for understanding and helpful ways to intervene.

You may also find in your journey that when you begin working with multiple providers, the opinions and types of information received will be quite varied. When you have a child with complex and puzzling behavior, it is quite common to find that no single provider has all the answers. As noted previously, providers approach the assessment of puzzling behavior based on their own particular philosophical orientation, as well as their training background and experiences. Thus, the feedback you receive can be quite different. Once you visit several professionals, it can be extremely challenging to put all the information together in order to decide on the best course of action. Since no one else in your child's life will be as committed as you, it will be up to you to put all of the information together into one coherent picture. This is not an easy task. At the end of this journey, your puzzle may be complete. Or your puzzle may still have pieces missing. In either case, you must move forward, and do the best you can.

A key factor in this process is to seek and be open to collaboration with other parents and professionals every step of the way. Each time you meet a new provider, encourage that person to communicate with the other professionals involved. When professionals and parents collaborate, the knowledge and strengths of each are maximized, and common ground can be established. For example, as a psychologist, I may say that a particular behavior difficulty is due to a child not receiving sufficient structure and feedback at home. An occupational therapist may say that the behavior is due to sensory difficulties. We may both be right or wrong. But when we begin speaking to one another, we begin to blend our thoughts to come up with a more inclusive way of thinking. When you are positive in your communications and when you encourage an atmosphere of collaboration, you are more likely to achieve a greater understanding of your child's behavior and more effective intervention strategies to address it. Collaboration is the key.

When All Else Fails

Children with puzzling behavior can be especially challenging, and intervention strategies frequently fail to produce any immediate noticeable effects. I have seen many parents go through a cycle of hopefulness and hopelessness. All parents of these children seem to go through ups and downs. Some days they feel like they are on top of things. Other days they feel depressed, as if nothing is getting any better, and they don't feel that they can cope. Remember that teachers and the children themselves can also move through this cycle. It is important to focus on the progress that has been made, on the little changes that have occurred, and on the information that has been gathered. Focus on the positive.

When all else fails, you sometimes must sit back, take a deep breath, and let nature take its course. No one can predict what is going to happen with a particular child. The variables are too extensive and complex. Remember the stories of very successful people who as children presented great challenges to their parents.[13] Again, think small, and appreciate the progress that has been made thus far. When you are ready, go seek more information. When you are ready, observe, think, and observe some more. Try to consider your child from a different perspective, and maintain or increase your collaboration with others. At the same time, remember to take care of yourself so that you do not get too stressed or burned out.

Most importantly, when all else fails, believe in your child. Believe in yourself as a parent. Believe that positive things can and will happen. One strategy that my mother has told me many times is to "bless my problems." No matter what is happening in my life, there is always someone in the world who has something happening that is even worse. Step back, and put things in perspective. Look for the positive,

---

[13] To read about the childhoods of famous people, the reader is encouraged to read the following resource: Goertzel, V., Goertzel, BA, Goertzel, T.G., Hansen, A. (2004). *Cradles of eminence: Childhoods of more than seven hundred famous men and women.* Scottsdale, AZ: Great Potential Press.

as well as the important lessons to be learned in your journey. Learn to appreciate the challenges you are facing and know that things can improve for the better. This strategy has helped me maintain my beliefs in working with children. It has helped me stay positive. It has given me hope. I have seen many miraculous changes happen during my career. It can happen to your child as well.

CHAPTER FIVE

Parent Resources

The following resource list includes books and websites that I have found particularly helpful in my work with children with behavioral, social, or learning challenges. No one specific resource has all the answers. Thus, in your quest to find help for your child, review several resources that have the potential to provide the answers to the questions you are asking. I have organized this list around topic areas for your convenience.

General Readings Related to Puzzling Behavior

Allen, K. E., & Marotz, L. R. (2006). *Developmental profiles: Pre-birth through twelve.* New York: Thomson Delmar Learning.

Axline, V. (1986). *Dibs in search of self.* New York: Ballantine.

Eide, B., & Eide, F. (2007). *The mislabeled child.* New York: Hyperion Press.

Gimpel, G. A., & Holland, M. (2003). *Emotional and behavioral problems of young children.* New York: Guilford.

Golding, W., & Epstein, E. (1959). *Lord of the flies.* New York: Perigee.

Greenspan, S. I. (1996). *The challenging child.* New York: Perseus.

Kauffman, J. (2005). *Characteristics of emotional and behavioral disorders of children and youth* (8th ed.). Upper Saddle River, NJ: Merrill Prentice Hall.

Klass, P., & Costello, E. (2004). *Quirky kids.* New York: Ballantine.

Kutscher, M. (2005). *Kids in the syndrome mix of ADHD, LD, Asperger's, Tourette's, Bipolar, and more!* Philadelphia: Jessica Kingsley Publishers.

Levine, M. (2002). *A mind at a time.* New York: Simon & Schuster.

Martin, A., Volkmar, F., & Lewis, M. (2007). *Child and adolescent psychiatry: A comprehensive textbook.* Philadelphia: Lippincott Williams and Wilkins.

Wicks-Nelson, R., & Israel, A. C. (2005). *Behavior disorders of childhood* (6th ed.). Columbus: Merrill Prentice Hall.

Assessment of Behavioral, Social, and Learning Challenges

American Psychiatric Association (2000). *Diagnostic and statistical book of mental disorders* (4th ed.). Text revision. Washington, DC: American Psychological Association.

Chandler, L. K., & Dahlquist, C. M. (2005). *Functional assessment: Strategies to prevent and remediate challenging behavior in school settings.* Columbus: Merrill Prentice Hall.

Schroeder, C. S. (2002). *Assessment and treatment of childhood problems.* New York: Guilford.

Home Interventions

Brazelton, B. (1992). *Touchpoints: Your child's emotional and behavioral development.* New York: Perseus.

Curwin, R. L., & Mendler, A. N. (1999). *Discipline with dignity.* Alexandria, VA: Association for Supervision and Curriculum Development.

Dobson, L. (2005). *The learning coach approach: Inspire, encourage, and guide your child toward greater success in school and in life.* Philadelphia: Running Press.

Dreikurs, R., Zuckerman, L., & Soltz, V. (1987). *Children: The challenge: The classic work on improving parent-child relations—intelligent, humane and eminently practical.* New York: Penguin.

Faber, A., & Mazlish, E. (1999). *How to talk so kids will listen & listen so kids will talk.* New York: HarperCollins.

Foster, C., & Fay, J. (2006). *Parenting with love and logic.* Colorado Springs, CO: Piñon Press.

Gordon, T. (2000). *Parent effectiveness training.* New York: Three Rivers Press.

Hart, L. (1995). *The winning family: Increasing self-esteem in your children and yourself.* Berkeley, CA: Celestial Arts Publishing.

Kircinka, M. S. (1998). *Raising your spirited child: A guide for parents whose child is more intense, sensitive, perceptive, persistent, energetic.* New York: HarperCollins.

MacKenzie, R. J. (2001). *Setting limits with your strong-willed child.* New York: Three Rivers Press.

McGraw, P. (2004). *Family first: Your step-by-step plan for creating a phenomenal family.* New York: Free Press.

McGraw, P. (2005). *The family first book: Specific tools, strategies and skills for creating a phenomenal family.* New York: Free Press.

Nelsen, J. (2006). *Positive discipline.* New York: Ballantine.

Patterson, G., & Forgatch, M. (1987). *Parents and adolescents living together.* Eugene, OR: Castalia Publishing.

Phelan, T. W. (2003). *1-2-3 Magic*. Glen Ellyn, IL: ParentMagic.

Rogers, F. (2002). *The Mister Rogers parenting book: Helping to understand your young child*. Philadelphia: Running Press.

Severe, S. (2003). *How to behave so your children will too*. New York: Penguin.

Steinberg, L. (2004). *The 10 basic principles of good parenting*. New York: Simon and Schuster.

Webster-Stratton, C. (2004). *The incredible years: A trouble-shooting guide for parents of children ages 2-8*. Seattle: Incredible Years.

Classroom Interventions

Alberto, P., & Troutman, A. (2003). *Applied behavior analysis for teachers* (6th ed.). Upper Saddle River, NJ: Merrill Prentice Hall.

Crone, D. A., Horner, R. H., & Hawken, L. S. (2004). *Responding to problem behavior in schools: The behavior education program*. New York: Guilford.

Curtis, S., Galbreath, H., & Curtis, J. (Eds.) (2005). *Teaching students with severe emotional and behavioral disorders: Best practices guide to intervention*. Olympia, WA: Office of the Superintendent of Public Instruction. (Available online at <www.k12.wa.edu>).

Hobbs, N. (1982). *The troubled and troubling child*. San Francisco: Jossey-Bass.

Jenson, W. R., Rhode, G., & Reavis, H. K. (2000). *Tough kid tool box*. Longmont, CO: Sopris West.

Jones, V., Dohrn, E., & Dunn, C. (2004). *Creating effective programs for students with emotional and behavioral disorders*. New York: Pearson.

Kohn, A. (1999). *Punished by rewards*. New York: Houghton Mifflin.

Naglieri, J. A., & Pickering, E. B. (2003). *Helping children learn: Intervention handouts for use in school and at home*. Baltimore: Brookes.

Nelson, J., Lott, L., & Glenn, S. (1997). *Positive discipline in the classroom*. Rocklin, CA: Prima.

Rhode, G., Jenson, W. R., & Reavis, H. K. (1996). *Tough kid book: Practical classroom management strategies*. Longmont, CO: Sopris West.

Shinn, M. R., Walker, H. M., & Stoner, G. (2002). *Interventions for academic and behavior problems II: Preventive and remedial approaches*. Bethesda, MD: National Association of School Psychologists.

Sugai, G., & Lewis, T. (1999). *Developing positive behavioral support for students with challenging behaviors*. Reston, VA: Council for Exceptional Children.

Thomas, A., & Grimes, J. (2002). *Best practices in school psychology IV (Volumes 1 and 2)*. Bethesda, MD: National Association of School Psychologists.

Walker, H. M. (1995). *The acting-out child: Coping with classroom disruption* (2nd ed.). Longmont, CO: Sopris West.

Walker, H. M., Ramsey, E., & Gresham, F. (2003). *Antisocial behavior in schools: Evidence-based practices (with InfoTrac)*. Belmont, CA: Wadsworth.

Specific Areas of Interest

ABUSE

Gil, E. (1991). *The healing power of play: Working with abused children*. New York: Guilford.

Gil, E., & Johnson, T. C. (1993). *Sexualized children: Assessment and treatment of sexualized children and children who molest*. Rockville, MD: Launch Press.

ANGER/EXPLOSIVE BEHAVIOR

Greene, R. W. (2005). *The explosive child*. New York: HarperCollins.

Greene, R. W. (2005). *Treating explosive kids: The collaborative problem-solving approach.* New York: Guilford.

Long, N., Wood, M., & Fecser, F. (2001). *Life space intervention: Talking with students in crisis.* Austin: Pro-Ed.

ATTENTION-DEFICIT/HYPERACTIVITY DISORDER (ADHD)

Barkley, R. (2000). *Taking charge of ADHD.* New York: Guilford.

Boylan, K. M. (2003). *Born to be wild: Freeing the spirit of the hyperactive child.* New York: Perigee.

Gantos, J. (1998). *Joey pigza swallowed the key.* New York: Harper-Collins.

Jensen, P. S. (2004). *Making the system work for your child with ADHD: How to cut through red tape and get what you need from doctors, teachers, schools, and health careplans.* New York: Guilford.

Monastra, V. (2005). *Parenting children with ADHD: 10 lessons that medicine cannot teach.* Washington, DC: American Psychological Association.

Rief, S. (2003). *The ADHD book of lists: A practical guide for helping children and teens with attention deficit disorders.* San Francisco: Jossey-Bass.

AUTISTIC DISORDER/ASPERGER'S DISORDER

Attwood, T. (2006). *The complete guide to Asperger's syndrome.* London: Jessica Kingsley Publishers.

Attwood, T. (1997). *Asperger's Syndrome: A guide for parents and professionals.* London: Jessica Kingsley Publishers.

Bondy, A., & Frost, L. (2002). *A picture's worth: PECS and other visual communication strategies in autism.* Bethesda, MD: Woodbine House.

Fling, E. (2000). *Eating an artichoke: A mother's perspective on Asperger Syndrome*. London: Jessica Kingsley Publishers.

Grandin, T. (2006). *Thinking in pictures*. New York: Knopf.

Greenspan, S. I. (1998). *The child with special needs: Encouraging intellectual and emotional growth*. Cambridge, MA: Perseus.

Greenspan, S. I. (2006). *Engaging autism: Helping children relate, communicate and think with the DIR floortime approach*. Cambridge, MA: Perseus.

Gutstein, S. E. (2000). *Solving the relationship puzzle*. Arlington, TX: Future Horizons.

Haddon, M. (2003). *The curious incident of the dog in the night-time*. New York: Random House.

Leaf, R., & McEachin, J. (1999). *A work in progress: Behavior management strategies and a curriculum for intensive behavioral treatment of autism*. New York: DRL Books.

Moyes, R. (2001). *Incorporating social goals in the classroom*. London: Jessica Kingsley Publishers.

National Research Council (2001). *Educating children with autism*. Washington, DC: National Academy of Sciences.

Schmidt, C., & Heybyrne, B. (2004). *Autism in the school-aged child: Expanding behavioral strategies and promoting success*. Denver, CO: Autism Family Press.

Sicile-Kira, C., & Grandin, T. (2005). *Autism spectrum disorders: The complete guide to understanding autism, Asperger's syndrome, pervasive developmental disorder, and other ASDs*. New York: Perigee.

Zysk, V., & Notbohm, E. (2004). *1001 great ideas for teaching and raising children with autism spectrum disorders*. Arlington, TX: Future Horizons.

CONDUCT DISORDER/DELINQUENT BEHAVIOR

Kazdin, A. (2005). *Parent management training: Treatment for oppositional, aggressive, and antisocial behavior in children and adolescents.* New York: Oxford University Press.

Patterson, G. R., Reid, J. B., & Dishion, T. J. (1992). *Antisocial boys.* Eugene, OR: Castalia.

Webster-Stratton, C. (1994). *Troubled families—problem children.* New York: Wiley.

DEPRESSION/ANXIETY

Aaron, E. (2003). *The highly sensitive child.* New York: HarperCollins.

Benson, H., & Klipper, M. (2000). *The relaxation response.* New York: HarperCollins.

Dacey, J. S., & Fiore, L. B. (2001). *Your anxious child.* San Francisco: Jossey-Bass.

Davis, M., Eshelman, E. R., & McKay, M. (2000). *The relaxation and stress reduction book.* Oakland, CA: New Harbinger Publications.

Merrell, K. W. (2001). *Helping students overcome depression and anxiety: A practical guide.* New York: Guilford.

Meichenbaum, D. (1985). *Stress inoculation training.* Elmsford, NY: Pergamon Press.

Seligman, M. E. (2002). *Authentic happiness.* New York: Free Press.

Seligman, M. E., Reivich, K., Jaycox, L., & Gilham, J. (1996). *The optimistic child: Proven program to safeguard children from depression and build lifetime resistance.* New York: HarperCollins.

Spence, S., Cobham, V., Wignall, A., & Rapee, R. M. (2000). *Helping your anxious child: A step-by-step guide for parents.* Oakland, CA: New Harbinger Publications.

DIVORCE

Emery, R. E. (2006). *The truth about divorce: Dealing with the emotions so you and your children can thrive.* New York: Plume.

FAMILY CONFLICT

Minuchin, S. (1974). *Families and family therapy.* Boston: Harvard University Press.

GENDER ISSUES

Coates, J., & Draves, W. (2006). *Smart boys, bad grades.* River Falls, NJ: Learning Resources Network. (Available at <www.lern.org>).

Gurian, M. (2005). *The minds of boys: Saving our sons from falling behind in school and life.* San Francisco: Jossey-Bass.

Sax, L. (2005). *Why gender matters: What parents and teachers need to know about the emerging science of sex differences.* New York: Random House.

Simmons, R. (2002). *Odd girl out: The hidden culture of aggression in girls.* New York: Harcourt.

Wiseman, R. (2002). *Queen bees and wannabees: Helping your daughter survive cliques, gossip, boyfriends, and other realities of adolescence.* New York: Three Rivers Press.

GIFTEDNESS

Davidson, J., & Davidson, B. (2004). *Genius denied: How to stop wasting our brightest young minds.* New York: Simon & Schuster.

Rogers, K. (2002). *Re-forming gifted education: How parents and teachers can match the program to the child.* Scottsdale, AZ: Great Potential Press.

Webb, J., Amend, E., Webb, N., Goerss, J., Beljan, P., & Olenchak, F. (2005). *Misdiagnosis and dual diagnosis of gifted children and adults.* Scottsdale, AZ: Great Potential Press.

Webb, J., Gore, J. L., & Amend, E. R. (2007). *A parent's guide to gifted children.* Scottsdale, AZ: Great Potential Press.

Winebrenner, S. (2001). *Teaching gifted kids in the regular classroom.* Minneapolis: Free Spirit Publishing.

HOME SCHOOLING

Rivero, L. (2002). *Creative home schooling: A resource guide for smart families.* Scottsdale, AZ: Great Potential Press.

HOMEWORK

Canter, L. (2005). *Homework without tears.* New York: HarperCollins.

Levine, M. (2003). *The myth of laziness.* New York: Simon & Schuster.

LEARNING DISABILITIES/DYSLEXIA

Bender, W. (2002). *Differentiating instruction for students with learning disabilities: Best teaching practices for general and special educators.* Thousand Oaks, CA: Corwin Press.

Mercer, C., & Mercer, A. (2004). *Teaching students with learning problems.* Upper Saddle River, NJ: Merrill Prentice Hall.

Rodis, P., Garrod, A., & Boscardin, M. L. (2001). *Learning disabilities and life stories.* Needham Heights, MA: Allyn and Bacon.

Shaywitz, S. (2005). *Overcoming dyslexia: A new and complete science-based program for reading problems at any level.* New York: Vintage.

Winebrenner, S. (1996). *Teaching kids with learning difficulties in the regular classroom.* Minneapolis: Free Spirit Publishing.

Wood, T. (2006). *Overcoming dyslexia for dummies*. Hoboken, NJ: Wiley.

SENSORY PROCESSING DISORDER

Auer, C. R., Blumberg, S., & Miller, L. J. (2006). *Parenting a child with sensory processing disorder: A family guide to understanding and supporting your sensory-sensitive child*. Oakland, CA: New Harbinger Publications.

Biel, L., & Peske, N. (2005). *Raising a sensory smart child*. New York: Penguin.

Kranowitz, C. S., & Miller, L. J. (2006). *The out-of-sync child: Recognizing and coping with sensory processing disorder*. New York: Perigee.

Smith, K. A., & Gouze, K. (2005). *The sensory-sensitive child*. New York: HarperCollins.

SOCIAL SKILLS

Brown, L. K., & Brown, M. (2001). *How to be a friend: A guide to making friends and keeping them*. New York: Little, Brown and Company.

Frankel, F., & Wetmore, B. (1996). *Good friends are hard to find: Help your child find, make, and keep friends*. Los Angeles: Perspective Publishing.

Goldstein, A., & McGinnis, E. (1997). *Skillstreaming the elementary school child: New strategies and perspectives for teaching prosocial skills* (2nd ed.). Champaign, IL: Research Press.

Gray, C. (2000). *The new social story book*. Arlington, TX: Future Horizons.

Moyes, R. A. (2003). *Incorporating social goals in the classroom: A guide for teachers and parents of children with high-functioning autism and Asperger Syndrome*. London: Jessica Kingsley Publishers.

OTHER AREAS OF INTEREST

Dorris, M. (1990). *The broken cord.* New York: HarperCollins.

Ferber, R. (2006). *Solve your child's sleep problems.* New York: Fireside.

Goertzel, V., Goertzel, M., Goertzel, T., Hansen, A. (2004). *Cradles of eminence: Childhoods of more than seven hundred famous men and women.* Scottsdale, AZ: Great Potential Press.

Klass, P., & Costello, E. (2003). *Quirky kids: Understanding and helping your child who doesn't fit in – when to worry and when not to worry.* New York: Ballantine Books.

Sommers-Flanagan, R., & Sommers-Flanagan, J. (2002). *Problem child or quirky kid?* Minneapolis, MN: Free Spirit Publishing.

Psychiatric Medication

PDR (2004). *Drug guide for mental health professionals.* Montvale, NJ: Thomson.

Preston, J., & Johnson, J. (2005). *Clinical psychopharmacology made ridiculously simple* (Medmaster series 2005). Miami: Medmaster.

Wilens, T. E. (2004). *Straight talk about psychiatric medications for kids.* New York: Guilford.

Special Education

Bateman, B., & Linden, M. A. (2006). *Better IEPs: How to develop legally correct and educationally useful programs.* Verona, WI: IEP Resources, Attainment Co.

Smith, D. D. (2006). *Introduction to special education.* New York: Allyn and Bacon.

Wright, P., & Wright, P. (2007). *Wrightslaw: Special education law.* Hartfield, VA: Harbor House Law Press. (Available at www.wrightslaw.com).

Meyer, D. J., & Vadasy, P. (2003). *Sibshops: Workshops for siblings of children with special needs.* Baltimore, MD: Brookes.

Websites[14]

Associates in Behavior and Child Development (ABCD): www. abcdseattle.com (clinic for children with behavioral, learning, and speech/language challenges).

Child and Adolescent Bipolar Foundation: www.cabf.org (information about children with bipolar disorder).

Childhood Anxiety Network: www.childhoodanxietynetwork.org (information about childhood anxiety).

Children and Adults with Attention-Deficit/Hyperactivity Disorder (CHADD): www.chadd.org (information about children and adults with ADHD).

Children's Institute for Learning Differences: www.childrens institute.com (school for children with behavioral, social, and learning challenges).

Eide Neurolearning Clinic: www.nearolearning.com (nationally renowned clinic for children with school or learning difficulties).

Foundation for Children with Behavioral Challenges: www. fcbcsupport.org (information about children with behavioral challenges).

Free Spirit Publishing: www.freespirit.com (self-help books for children and parents).

Future Horizons: www.futurehorizons-autism.com (books on Autistic Disorder/Asperger's Disorder).

Great Potential Press: www.giftedbooks.com (resources about gifted children).

Hoagies' Gifted Education Page: www.hoagiesgifted.org (information about children who are considered gifted and/or who are gifted and have some type of learning challenge [dual exceptionality]).

---

[14] Additional websites for each type of professional are located in Table 2.

International Dyslexia Association: www.interdys.org (information about children with Dyslexia).

LD Online: www.ldonline.org (information about children with learning disabilities and ADHD).

Lifespan Psychological Services: www.lifespanps.com (clinic for children and adults with emotional, learning, or speech/language challenges).

National Alliance on Mental Illness (NAMI): www.nami.org (information about children with mental illness).

Nonverbal Learning Disability Association (NLDA): www.nlda.org (information about Nonverbal Learning Disorder).

Outofsyncchild.com: www.outofsyncchild.com (information on ADHD and child behavior).

Russell A. Barkley, PhD—The Official Site: www.russellbarkley.org (information on ADHD).

SchwabLearning.org: www.schwablearning.org (information about helping children with learning difficulties).

Sensory Processing Disorder Network: www.sinetwork.org (information about Sensory Processing Disorder).

Society for Developmental and Behavioral Pediatrics: www.sdbp.org (current research and intervention about children with special needs).

StrugglingTeens.com: www.strugglingteens.com (therapeutic educational programs for children with emotional, behavioral, and other difficulties).

Supporting the Emotional Needs of the Gifted (SENG): www.sengifted.org (information about children who are gifted and need emotional support).

The Arc: www.thearc.org (information about children with intellectual and developmental disabilities).

The Source: www.maapservices.org (information about Autism Spectrum Disorders).

Tourette Syndrome Association (TSA): www.tsa-usa.org (information about Tourette Syndrome).

Wrightslaw: www.wrightslaw.com (information about special education law and advocacy).

Glossary of Terms

ACCOMMODATIONS

Teaching supports that a child requires to successfully learn in the classroom. Examples of accommodations are providing the child with additional time to take tests, allowing the child with written language difficulties to dictate answers, or providing the child with attention difficulties preferential seating in the front of the classroom. The term "modification" is used when the curriculum is actually changed – see the definition of "modifications" below.

ADD

See Attention-Deficit/Hyperactivity Disorder.

ADHD

See Attention-Deficit/Hyperactivity Disorder.

ANTECEDENTS

A term used while conducting a functional behavioral assessment to refer to environmental events that immediately precede the behavior of concern. For example, an antecedent to an angry outburst could be "being told what to do."

ANXIETY

State of arousal, fear, or tension, which everyone experiences at one time or another. At times, significant and persistent anxiety can be characterized as an "Anxiety Disorder." See description of Anxiety Disorders below.

ANXIETY DISORDERS

A grouping of clinical disorders described in the Diagnostic and Statistical Manual of Mental Disorders-IV-TR (DSM-IV-TR) that have anxiety as a key component. Examples of anxiety disorders include Specific Phobia, Generalized Anxiety Disorder, Posttraumatic Stress Disorder, and Obsessive-Compulsive Disorder. See description of each disorder elsewhere in this glossary.

ASPERGER'S DISORDER

A condition that is part of a larger diagnostic category called "Autism Spectrum Disorders" or "Pervasive Developmental Disorders." Children with Asperger's Disorder have severe and sustained impairments in social interaction. They also have challenges with restricted, repetitive patterns of behavior, interests, and activities. The defining criteria of Asperger's Disorder may be found in the Diagnostic and Statistical Manual of Mental Disorders-IV-TR (DSM-IV-TR).

ATTENTION-DEFICIT/HYPERACTIVITY DISORDER (ADHD)

A Disruptive Behavior Disorder that is characterized by hyperactivity, impulsivity, and inattention. Symptoms in these core areas must be present early in life and must impact a child's functioning. This is a common diagnosis for children who have difficulty sitting still, completing tasks, or concentrating at school. The term "ADD" or Attention-Deficit Disorder is from a prior edition of the Diagnostic and Statistical Manual of Mental Disorders. This term is still widely used among the general public to indicate that a child has attention difficulties but is not demonstrating significant behavioral challenges. The defining criteria of ADHD may be found in the Diagnostic and Statistical Manual of Mental Disorders-IV-TR (DSM-IV-TR).

AUDITORY-TYPE INFORMATION

Information that is received through the auditory system (i.e., ears). A lecture given by a teacher is an example of auditory-type information being delivered to the student. Some people learn best by listening. Others learn best by seeing. Some people have challenges with learning through hearing. If a deficit is found in the auditory system, they may have trouble learning information delivered through sounds alone.

AUTISTIC DISORDER (AUTISM)

A Pervasive Developmental Disorder that is characterized by impairments in social interaction and communication skills. Children with

Autistic Disorder also have restricted and repetitive patterns of behavior, interests, and activities. The defining criteria of Autistic Disorder may be found in the Diagnostic and Statistical Manual of Mental Disorders-IV-TR (DSM-IV-TR).

BIPOLAR DISORDER

A Mood Disorder characterized by cyclical periods of depression and mania. The defining criteria of Bipolar Disorder may be found in the Diagnostic and Statistical Manual of Mental Disorders-IV-TR (DSM-IV-TR).

BREAKDOWN POINTS

The specific points where a child's learning goes awry. This is a concept Dr. Mel Levine uses in his book *A Mind at a Time*. He notes that a good assessment should isolate specific breakdown points so that strategies can be used to address challenges. For example, in reading, a breakdown point could be not being able to identify certain letters. In written language, a breakdown point could be that the child has difficulty coming up with her own ideas.

CENTRAL AUDITORY PROCESSING DISORDER (CAPD)

A disorder in how auditory information is processed in the brain. It is not due to a hearing impairment. Instead, individuals with CAPD have normal hearing but have difficulty understanding certain auditory information presented to them.

COGNITION

Learning and thinking.

COGNITIVE PROCESSING DISORDER

A disorder, or learning challenge, in which intelligence is normal, yet despite this normal intelligence, a child has difficulty applying what he or she knows. Or, a child with this disorder may take much more time to demonstrate what he or she knows. Typically, a child with a Cognitive Processing Disorder does not do well on timed tests. Instead, more time is needed to complete the same amount of items as other students have completed in a shorter amount of time.

COMMUNICATION DISORDER

A disorder that is characterized by impairment in some aspects of speech or language skills. Examples of Communication Disorders include Expressive Language Disorders, Mixed Expressive-Receptive Language Disorders, Phonological Disorders, and Stuttering. Each of these disorders is defined elsewhere in this glossary. The defining criteria of Communication Disorders may be found in the Diagnostic and Statistical Manual of Mental Disorders-IV-TR (DSM-IV-TR).

CONDUCT DISORDER

A Disruptive Behavior Disorder in which a child engages in behavior that persistently violates the rights of others in some way. A young person with a Conduct Disorder may be aggressive toward others. Another person with a Conduct Disorder may steal, destroy property, or seriously violate the rules in some manner. The defining criteria of conduct disorder may be found in the Diagnostic and Statistical Manual of Mental Disorders-IV-TR (DSM-IV-TR).

CONSEQUENCES

A term used while conducting a functional behavioral assessment, to refer to environmental events that immediately follow the behavior of concern. For example, a consequence of persistent angry behavior could be that the child loses all of his friends.

CULTURAL FACTORS

Factors that affect the development of psychopathology and that are related to a person's cultural background. For example, sometimes children from different cultures are diagnosed early in their lives as having speech/language disorders. However, children from certain cultures may begin to speak later than others because early verbalization may not necessarily be encouraged. Thus, depending on the cultural norms, a child at 4 years of age may or may not necessarily have a disorder. A quality assessment of a child must always include examination of cultural factors that could be at play.

DAILY LIVING SKILLS

These include skills such as dressing, bathing, eating, socialization, and dealing with money.

DEMYSTIFICATION

A process through which the child discovers the characteristics of his/her profile. In this guide, I have recommended that parents develop a profile of "strengths and weaknesses" for their child. This is a concept Dr. Mel Levine uses in his book *A Mind at a Time*. Dr. Levine calls this a neurodevelopmental profile. Once a child understands his or her developmental profile, he/she is more likely to perform better at school.

DEVELOPMENTAL PSYCHOPATHOLOGY

An approach to the study of behavioral and emotional difficulties in children that combines the fields of psychopathology and developmental psychology. The aim is to understand the central mechanisms of what causes a child to engage in or acquire a particular type of disorder or difficulty. The field of developmental psychopathology takes information from a variety of disciplines and philosophies in order to look for "truths."

DIAGNOSTIC AND STATISTICAL MANUAL OF MENTAL DISORDERS (DSM-IV-TR)

A manual that contains the diagnostic criteria for a comprehensive set of "mental disorders" or forms of psychopathology. It was completed by a number of workgroups and is published by the American Psychiatric Association. Mental health clinicians use this manual in their practice for diagnoses and research.

DISRUPTIVE BEHAVIOR DISORDERS

Disorders that are considered more externalizing in nature. Types of Disruptive Behavior Disorders include Attention-Deficit/Hyperactivity Disorder, Conduct Disorder, and Oppositional Defiant Disorder. Each of these disorders is described elsewhere in this glossary. The defining criteria of Disruptive Behavior Disorders may be found in the Diagnostic and Statistical Manual of Mental Disorders-IV-TR (DSM-IV-TR).

DYSLEXIA

A specific learning disability that is considered neurological in origin. Dyslexia is often characterized by challenges in word recognition, poor spelling, and difficulties with decoding. Most Dyslexia typically results from a deficit in phonological processing (i.e., the ability to distinguish between different sounds).

DYSTHYMIC DISORDER

A type of Mood Disorder that is characterized by a depressed mood for most of the day, for most days, and for at least 1 year for children. The defining criteria of Dysthymic Disorder may be found in the Diagnostic and Statistical Manual of Mental Disorders-IV-TR (DSM-IV-TR).

ECHOLALIA

Repeating over and over what other people say.

ELECTROMYOGRAPHY (EMG)

A test that examines the health of the muscles and the nerves.

ELECTROENCEPHALOGRAPHY (EEG)

A test that measures the electrical activity of the brain (i.e., brain-waves).

EMOTIONAL INTELLIGENCE

A type of intelligence that refers to the ability to understand and express emotions effectively.

EMOTIONAL REGULATION

The ability to regulate one's emotions.

EXECUTIVE FUNCTIONING

The brain's ability to gather information, make interpretations, and make decisions based upon the inputted information. Children may have difficulties with executive functioning if they have difficulties with attention or controlling their impulses. Neuropsychological testing is indicated if there are concerns about executive functioning.

EXPRESSIVE LANGUAGE DISORDER

A Communication Disorder in which the child has difficulty expressing herself with verbal language. The defining criteria of Expressive Language Disorder may be found in the Diagnostic and Statistical Manual of Mental Disorders-IV-TR (DSM-IV-TR).

EXTINCTION BURST

A term meaning that the behavior of concern often gets worse before it gets better.

FINE MOTOR SKILLS

Small muscle movements in the fingers, in coordination with the eyes.

FLUENCY

Being able to quickly and accurately complete a particular task. For example, a person has good reading fluency when he/she can read quickly and accurately. Language fluency describes when a person can quickly articulate words and sentences in an effective manner. Good fluency is generally a reliable indication that a person has good speed of information processing.

FUNCTIONAL BEHAVIORAL ASSESSMENT

A term from the field of applied behavioral analysis to refer to the process of determining the cause (or "function") of a behavior of concern. A functional behavioral assessment helps to form a hypothesis for the behavior so that an appropriate intervention may be developed and implemented.

GENERALIZATION

When learned behavior, skills, and/or emotions are exhibited across settings and situations.

GENERALIZED ANXIETY DISORDER

An Anxiety Disorder characterized by excessive anxiety and worry that causes much turmoil in a person's life. The source of the anxiety is often unknown. The defining criteria of Generalized Anxiety Disorder may be found in the Diagnostic and Statistical Manual of Mental Disorders-IV-TR (DSM-IV-TR).

GIFTED

A term to refer to the cognitive strengths of a child. There is no universally accepted definition of what is considered gifted. The most common definition is that a child is considered gifted when he or she has achieved a score on an intelligence test above 130. This score is two or more standard deviations above the mean. Psychologists typically provide the assessment in this area.

GROSS MOTOR SKILLS

The ability to use large muscles (e.g., in the legs, arms) in a coordinated fashion to do such activities as walking, running, jumping, throwing a ball, etc. Occupational and physical therapists are typically called upon to provide assessment in this area.

HYPOTHESIS TESTING

A hypothesis is a proposed reason that explains some type of phenomenon of study. In this guide, hypothesis testing refers to the process of investigating proposed reasons for puzzling behavior. When attempting to understand puzzling behavior, it is best to form an initial hypothesis about why a child does what he or she does. Then, this hypothesis is used to guide future interventions and assessment.

INDIVIDUALS WITH DISABILITIES EDUCATION ACT (IDEA)

The IDEA is a federal law that protects the rights of students with disabilities. The IDEA is the foundation of what is currently known as "special education" in today's public schools.

LEARNED HELPLESSNESS

A pattern of behavior in which the individual feels helpless to work through challenges on his or her own.

LEARNING DISABILITY

Learning disabilities generally refer to challenges in the ability to understand or use spoken or written language, read, do mathematical calculations, or complete mathematically-based problems. The term "learning disability" is one of the disability categories in the Individuals with Disabilities Education Act (IDEA) and is used frequently in public schools.

LEARNING DISORDER

A disorder in which a child's skills in reading, written language, or mathematics is substantially lower than that expected, given the child's age, schooling, and level of intellectual ability. The term "Learning Disorder" is used interchangeably with the term "Learning Disability" and "Dyslexia." The term "Learning Disorder" is from the Diagnostic and Statistical Manual of Mental Disorders-IV-TR (DSM-IV-TR).

MAGNETIC RESONANCE IMAGING (MRI)

A medical procedure used to scan inside the human body in order to assess for possible medical difficulties.

MAJOR DEPRESSIVE DISORDER

A Mood Disorder characterized by significant depression over a period of several weeks. The defining criteria of Major Depressive Disorder may be found in the Diagnostic and Statistical Manual of Mental Disorders-IV-TR (DSM-IV-TR).

MENTAL RETARDATION

A cognitive delay that is characterized by below-average intellectual ability and is accompanied by limitations in adaptive behavior (e.g., self-care, communication, life skills at home, or social skills). Severe Mental Retardation is often diagnosed early in childhood, since the child is not achieving developmental milestones on time. Mild Mental Retardation is often diagnosed later in childhood after assessment with an intellectual test and adaptive behavior scales indicates that the child is functioning in the below-average range. The definition and description of types of mental retardation may also be found in the Diagnostic and Statistical Manual of Mental Disorders-IV-TR (DSM-IV-TR).

MIXED RECEPTIVE-EXPRESSIVE LANGUAGE DISORDER

When a child has both receptive and expressive difficulties, this child is said to have a Mixed Receptive-Expressive Language Disorder. This Receptive-Expressive Language Disorder is described in the Diagnostic and Statistical Manual of Mental Disorders-IV-TR (DSM-IV-TR).

MODIFICATIONS

A term commonly used to refer to classroom curriculum changes in order to better individualize the instruction for a child. Examples of modifications include reducing the number of math problems, allowing a child with written language difficulties to write only one paragraph rather than the required five paragraphs, and teaching daily living skills to a child with developmental delays rather than requiring the child to be taught the mainstream curriculum. The term "accommodations" is used when the curriculum stays the same but added supports are provided for the student to help him or her better access the curriculum. See the definition of "accommodations" above.

MOOD DISORDER

A disorder in which a disturbance of mood is the predominant feature. Examples of Mood Disorders include Major Depressive Disorder, Dysthymic Disorder, and Bipolar Disorder. Each of these mood disorders is defined elsewhere in this glossary. The defining criteria of

Mood Disorder may be found in the Diagnostic and Statistical Manual of Mental Disorders-IV-TR (DSM-IV-TR).

NATURALISTIC OBSERVATION

A method of observation whereby someone is observed in a natural setting and under natural conditions. When a naturalistic observation is done on a child, the observer watches the child in natural conditions and notes without judgment all that is seen.

NEURODEVELOPMENTAL PROFILES

A term to refer to the strengths and weaknesses of each child in order to determine why he or she has trouble learning. This is a concept Dr. Mel Levine uses in his book *A Mind at a Time*. All children have a unique profile of skills is such areas as memory, language, and attention. A challenge in one or more of these areas could lead to academic delays.

NEUROPSYCHOLOGICAL TESTING

An assessment in which a battery of tests is given to a person suspected of having neurological dysfunction. The results of the tests can provide information about how the person is performing in certain areas. Neuropsychological testing is most commonly completed by a board certified clinical neuropsychologist.

NORMS

Measurements of a large group of people that are used for comparing the scores of an individual with those of the group.

OBSESSIVE-COMPULSIVE DISORDER (OCD)

An Anxiety Disorder that is characterized by obsessions (i.e., recurrent thoughts that cannot be suppressed) and compulsions (i.e., repetitive patterns of behavior). The defining criteria of Obsessive-Compulsive Disorder may be found in the Diagnostic and Statistical Manual of Mental Disorders-IV-TR (DSM-IV-TR).

OPPOSITIONAL DEFIANT DISORDER

A disorder in which the child is persistently negative, defiant, disobedient, or hostile toward people of authority. The defining criteria of Oppositional Defiant Disorder may be found in the Diagnostic and Statistical Manual of Mental Disorders-IV-TR (DSM-IV-TR).

PERVASIVE DEVELOPMENTAL DISORDER

A disorder with origins in early childhood that are characterized by significant impairment in several areas: social interaction; communication; and/or the presence of stereotyped behavior, interests, and activities. Clinicians often use the term "Autism Spectrum Disorders" interchangeably with this term. Examples of a Pervasive Developmental Disorder include Autistic Disorder and Asperger's Disorder. The defining criteria of Pervasive Developmental Disorder may be found in the Diagnostic and Statistical Manual of Mental Disorders-IV-TR (DSM-IV-TR).

PHONOLOGICAL DISORDER

A Communication Disorder in which a child has difficulty using expected speech sounds. The defining criteria of phonological disorder may be found in the Diagnostic and Statistical Manual of Mental Disorders-IV-TR (DSM-IV-TR).

POSITIVE BEHAVIORAL SUPPORT (PBS)

A system-wide and proactive method in which behavioral challenges in a school are prevented or responded to with data-based decision making.

POSTTRAUMATIC STRESS DISORDER

An Anxiety Disorder characterized by repeated re-experiencing of traumatic events through distressing thoughts, dreams, flashbacks, or hallucinations. The defining criteria of Posttraumatic Stress Disorder may be found in the Diagnostic and Statistical Manual of Mental Disorders-IV-TR (DSM-IV-TR).

PROBLEM-SOLVING APPROACH

A step-by-step procedure that helps to clarify concerns and to systematically investigate possible causes for the behavioral, social, or learning challenges that you see in your child.

PROCESSING SPEED

A term used to describe how quickly a child processes information. Children have difficulty quickly understanding directions or producing written material in a prompt matter because their overall ability to process information is slow and painstaking.

PROFILE-BASED APPROACH

An intervention approach in which the parents use information about their child to create an effective intervention plan that will address both the areas of need as well as areas of strength.

PSYCHOPATHOLOGY

Behaviors/emotions that are considered abnormal. Psychopathology is often synonymous with the term "mental illness."

PSYCHOTIC DISORDERS

Disorders in which a person experiences delusions or hallucinations. The most common type of Psychotic Disorder is Schizophrenia. The defining criteria of Psychotic Disorder may be found in the Diagnostic and Statistical Manual of Mental Disorders-IV-TR (DSM-IV-TR).

PUZZLING BEHAVIOR

A term used frequently throughout this guide to initially describe children with behavioral, social, and/or learning challenges. The term is used when a comprehensive understanding of the child has not yet been developed. Here the term "puzzling" only implies that something about the child's behavior seems unusual in comparison to other children's behavior. The child with puzzling behavior may have a legitimate disorder or may not have anything wrong.

RECEPTIVE LANGUAGE DISORDER

A Communication Disorder in which a child has difficulty understanding aspects of spoken language.

REINFORCEMENT

Something that is given to the child that increases a particular behavior; this is considered positive reinforcement. Negative reinforcement is when something that is taken away that results in an increase in a particular behavior.

RESILIENCY FACTORS

Characteristics that protect an individual from developing psychopathology. An example of a resiliency factor is a child having many positive relationships. The relationships may help protect the child from developing significant difficulties.

RISK FACTORS

Characteristics that increase the risk of an individual developing psychopathology. For example, a risk factor for a child developing depression is lack of social support at home or school. If someone feels isolated, he/she is more prone to depression. Risk factors can be biological, environmental, or social.

RULE OUT

A term that is used by clinicians to indicate that more investigation of a certain possible causal factor is needed. For example, if a physician states that she needs to "rule out" thyroid problems as a possible cause of depression, this means that the physician needs to investigate whether thyroid problems are present.

SCAFFOLDING

An instructional technique in which the child is provided with strong supports as he or she acquires a new skill. As the skill is mastered, the supports are systematically reduced and eventually removed.

SCHIZOPHRENIA

A type of Psychotic Disorder in which an individual has impairments in perception. A person with Schizophrenia may demonstrate disorganized thinking, delusions, or hallucinations. The defining criteria of Schizophrenia may be found in the Diagnostic and Statistical Manual of Mental Disorders-IV-TR (DSM-IV-TR).

SECOND LANGUAGE ACQUISITION

A term to note that a child is acquiring another language in addition to his/her native language.

SEIZURE DISORDERS

Uncoordinated electrical discharges that spread throughout the brain. Epilepsy is a Seizure Disorder.

SENSORY PROCESSING DISORDER

A neurological disorder that is manifested by processing difficulties in a number of sensory areas (e.g., vision, auditory, movement). Sensory information is received but may be processed abnormally. Sensory Processing Disorder, formally called Sensory Integration Disorder, is typically diagnosed and treated by an occupational therapist.

SETTING EVENTS (DISTANT EVENTS)

A term used in functional behavioral assessment to refer to environmental events that precede the behavior of concern at some point in time. Setting events usually occur before antecedent events, which immediately precede the behavior. Setting events can also be events that occur concurrently with the antecedent event. Examples of these events include hunger, thirst, fatigue, or mood issues.

SLEEP APNEA

A Sleep Disorder that is characterized by breathing pauses during sleep.

SOCIAL COGNITIVE PROCESSING

The ability to accurately pick up and understand social cues in the environment.

SOCIAL SKILLS

Skills that allow one to effectively interact and establish meaningful relationships with others.

SPECIFIC PHOBIA

An Anxiety Disorder that is characterized by a persistent fear of an object or situation (e.g., fear of insects). The defining criteria of Specific Phobia may be found in the Diagnostic and Statistical Manual of Mental Disorders-IV-TR (DSM-IV-TR).

STEREOTYPIC

A term describing repetitive and habitual types of behaviors.

STRENGTH-BASED APPROACH

An approach in which interventions build or enhance the identified strengths of a child. For example, if a child with social difficulties and no friends also plays violin, a strength-based approach to intervention would have a goal of increasing the level of competence on violin.

STRESSORS

Events that happen to a person that create a "stress reaction." Stressors can be daily hassle-type events, such as having a flat tire when rushing to work. Stressors can also be major life events, such as the death of a loved one. Stressors can be both positive and negative since each type of situation can produce a stress reaction.

STRESS REACTION

Reaction to a stressor. The reaction can be physiological or psychological. For example, if a child has to change schools, a possible stress reaction could be an increase of angry outbursts. The type of stress reaction is dependent on the type of stressor and the person's interpretation of the stressor. A change of schools for one child may be positive and cause stress due to overexcitement. The change of schools for another child may be negative and result in more angry behavior.

STUTTERING

A Communication Disorder in which the child has difficulties with verbal fluency and time patterning of speech. The defining criteria of Stuttering may be found in the Diagnostic and Statistical Manual of Mental Disorders-IV-TR (DSM-IV-TR).

SUMMARY STATEMENTS

Statements used to summarize the findings of a functional behavioral assessment. Summary statements include a description of the factors surrounding the cause of a behavior of concern and a statement of what the function of the behavior is hypothesized to be.

TARGET BEHAVIOR

The behavior of concern that is the focus of intervention.

TEMPERAMENT

Innate, genetically-based aspects of an individual's personality. Some children, for example, are born with a predisposition to be anxious.

TERATOGEN

Any agent (e.g., medication, chemical, disease) that may interfere with the normal development of the fetus.

TRANSITION

Moving from one place or activity to another.

VISUAL DISCRIMINATION

Skill in discriminating small visual images.

VISUAL-SPATIAL LEARNER

A child who learns best when the content is seen. This child tends to think in pictures and in a holistic fashion.

Index

About the Author

 Dr. Curtis has extensive training and over 25 years of experience in working with children demonstrating behavioral, social, and learning challenges. He began his studies in psychology at the University of California, Los Angeles in 1975. He later completed his PhD at Utah State University in 1992 in professional-scientific psychology. This program was approved by the American Psychological Association in Clinical, Counseling, and School Psychology. At Utah State University, he received training in both child clinical and school psychology.

Photo taken by Nick Felkey

He completed a predoctoral internship and postdoctoral fellow-ship in child clinical psychology in the Department of Psychiatry and Behavioral Sciences at the University of Washington School of Medicine in 1993. Since completion of his formal academic training, he has worked in inpatient, outpatient, and school settings. He was the special education director at Seattle University from 2001 to 2006. Dr. Curtis now engages in full-time private practice with Lifespan.